For Werner a
friendship, wishing you long
life

ACADEMIC
STUDIES
PRESS

The Righteous
of the Wehrmacht

Simon Malkes

Translated from the French
by Lilyana Yankova

Boston • 2015

Library of Congress Cataloging-in-Publication Data:
A catalog record for this book as available from the Library of Congress.

ISBN 978-1-61811-449-5 (paperback)
ISBN 978-1-61811-455-6 (electronic)

Cover design by Ivan Grave

Published by Academic Studies Press in 2015

28 Montfern Avenue
Brighton, MA 02135, USA
press@academicstudiespress.com
www.academicstudiespress.com

I dedicate this book

to my daughter, Nathalie,

her husband, Jean-Michel,

and their children, Jeremy and Clara.

Contents

Introduction   8
Serge Klarsfeld

Preface   12

Names Concordance   13

1 My Childhood in Wilno and Holszany   14
(1930-1939)

2 The War: The Soviet Occupation   29
(1939-1941)

3 The War: The German Occupation   34
(1941-1944)

4 The HKP   47
(1943-1944)

5 Liberation, Vilnius, and Lodz   56
(1944-1949)

6 University Years in Munich   60
(1949-1952)

7 Paris   66
(1952-1961)

8 Work, Family, and Homeland   71
(1961-2012)

9 Major Karl Plagge   84
(1897-1957)

Appendix   99

Acknowledgements   107

Index   108

Introduction

Simon Malkes's account is first and foremost the story of a family in the bloody Holocaust nightmare in Vilna (Vilnius), where, thanks to a senior Wehrmacht officer's surprisingly positive attitude toward Jews, Simon's family and some hundred other Jews survived.

Simon was fourteen years old in 1941. He waited for a long time after his retirement to undertake a thorough investigation and all the steps necessary to pay the tribute that his German savior, Karl Plagge, deserved. Perhaps it is the success of Simon's personal and professional life that gave rise to this belated recognition in the form of solemn posthumous awarding of the Righteous Medal to Karl Plagge in Jerusalem in 2005. When Karl Plagge died in 1957, it was still too early for survivors to look for him and thank him. Europe after the war bristled with borders that were difficult to cross. Holocaust survivors tried to rebuild their lives in Europe, Israel, the United States, or elsewhere. Time was necessary for a group of survivors to realize that their lives had been saved by the German officer and that he had done so unselfishly, out of pure humanism. Although he had been a member of the Nazi party since 1931 and indeed had voted for Hitler, he had not voted for the Holocaust. Under the Third Reich, there were Nazis who were not vicious, and executioners who were not members of the Party. Karl Plagge chose to remain human.

Following Germany's invasion of the Soviet Union and the Baltic states, Plagge was appointed commander of a workshop for repairing military vehicles in Vilnius, Lithuania. He was a 44-year-old mechanical engineer who had fought in World War One. He employed not only Germans, but also about 500 Jews who were amazed to find themselves and their families safe in Plagge's workshop, where they received decent amounts of food and Germans' attitude contrasted with the outburst of violence that had poured down upon Vilna Jews, almost all of whom were taken to Ponary forest and its mass graves. The Vilna Jewish community was erased. The Jerusalem of the North was a community that had stood out with its intellectual and spiritual resistance as well as with its heroes, such as Yitzhak Wittenberg, who surrendered to the SS in order to avoid repressions and committed suicide with cyanide; Abba Kowner, his successor, the poet Avrom Suzkewer, and Yitzhak Arad, who later became an Israeli general, then president of Yad Vashem.

Plagge insisted upon the indispensability of the accomplished work and his Jewish workers' competence, which allowed him skillfully to keep them with him despite the SS's willingness to get rid of all Jews, regardless of their utility to the war economy.

Plagge's great merit further consists in having personally taken Simon's mother to the hospital where she could remain safe for several months until Vilna's liberation. The rescuer's deed persuaded Yad Vashem to award the Righteous Medal to a German officer and member of the Nazi party, a Vilna Schindler of sorts.

Shortly before liberation, when Plagge warned his protégés that the army was about to retreat and that they would have to face the SS and their Lithuanian accomplices, Simon, his father, and a few friends' families took refuge in a hideout prepared in anticipation of the event. They crowded in together, but the conditions soon became so unbearable that they had to kill with their bare hands and in front of their children a man and his wife who panicked and lost their minds, putting them all in danger of death.

In July 1944, the Soviets seized Vilna. A new life began, which is still going on for Simon in 2014. Here lies one of this Holocaust account's major strengths: it does not end when freedom comes to replace tyranny, but rather goes on to tell us what the seventeen-year-old boy did with his life. He was one of the rare survivors to have been saved (along with his parents) thanks to Karl Plagge. Did not such a happy ending require a special commitment on behalf of the survivor to justify the miracle? Simon's contemporaries have apparently set their minds and energy on a very simple cause: "I survived for a reason and I will do everything possible to become a man."

I shall not refer to others since Simon's case suffices. He grew up in the 1930s in a well-to-do environment and spoke Yiddish, Hebrew, and Polish as a child. He then learned German during the three years of occupation. Simon began his studies in engineering in Lodz (1947-1949) and completed them in Munich (1949-1952). A most dutiful son, he then joined his parents, who had moved to Paris, and learned French. Later, after he had become a highly qualified electrical engineer and traveled abroad regularly, English became his working language. Simon never ceased studying, advancing, and innovating. Once retired, he volunteered to work for ORT, an educational institution that teaches a number of technical professions and which has done so much for poor Jews worldwide.

As soon as he retired, Simon had the chance to think about the Odyssey that his life has been and to realize that what he owes to the German major should be shared with the world. People should know about Plagge and his example should shine as a beacon of light through the dark window of the Vilna Holocaust. The adolescents who once worked at the workshop and repaired German military trucks have once again gathered together despite long distances, thanks largely to the internet.

They have reconstructed Plagge's personality and career. They write, publish, and thus manage to take him out of anonymity and make him a model as he rightfully deserves, as one can judge from a letter he sent in 1948 to the only survivor who contacted him at the time: "How strange and mysterious are the roads along which life takes us. I constantly think and dream about the people I used to be so close to at that difficult time: where could the people who have grown so dear to my heart be today?"

He too has grown in those people's hearts, as they have demonstrated. Karl Plagge is today a rare and exemplary German for the Jewish people. Those whose lives he has saved have in turn saved him from an anonymous and definitive death.

Plagge's posthumous life will be valuable and fruitful.

Serge Klarsfeld

Preface

I spent my childhood and adolescence in Poland, which is why the names of cities, streets, and people in this book are all in Polish. The reader will find a small names concordance below that will guide him in his reading of Polish names.

I hope that my unpretentious work, which will take no more than a few hours to read, will help you learn and understand what happened in Northeastern Europe between 1939 and 1944, first during the Soviet occupation, and then under the Nazis.

Before World War II, Wilno was a semi-holy city that Napoleon Bonaparte used to call the "Jerusalem of the North" and that Jewish people referred to as "the Jerusalem of Lita." The city set an example throughout the Jewish world with its culture and secular as well as religious education. Of the 65,000 Jews who resided there before the Holocaust, only between 200 and 300 survived, while the Jewish culture has been entirely erased from the earth.

I owe my life to Major Karl Plagge of the Wehrmacht, for whom I managed to procure posthumously the Righteous Among the Nations Medal in 2004. Only two percent of a total of over 20,200 Righteous are of German origin.

Names Concordance

Polish	English
Badasz	Badash
Gerszon	Guershon
Grisza	Grisha
Holszany	Holshany
Jagmin	Yagmin
Mickiewicz	Mitskiewitsh
Riwkes	Rivkes
Riwa	Riva
Sutzkewer	Sutzkever
Zawalna	Zavalna
Trocka	Trotzka
Wojczyk	Voytshik
Lukiszki	Lukishki
Genichowicz	Guenihovitsh
Slowacki	Slovatski

Chapter One
My Childhood in Wilno and Holszany (1930–1939)

I was born in Wilno, Poland. Unlike Paris or London, Wilno has often changed rulers over the centuries. It has been Lithuanian, Russian, Polish, German, Russian again, and finally Lithuanian once more today. Every new occupier quickly altered the city's name: the Polish *Wilno* became *Vilna* in Russian, *Wilna* in German, and *Vilnius* in Lithuanian. The Yiddish *Vilne*, however, persisted throughout the centuries. My grandparents and my parents were all born there in the Tsarist era. We spoke three languages: Russian, Yiddish, and Polish.

My father, Abram Malkes, and my mother Rasia, née Badasz, met in Wilno in 1924-1925. After the wedding, they settled down at 14 Zawalna Street. My father's shop for electrical appliances was around the corner, on Great Pogulanka Street. His job suited him perfectly while he was single: he was making good profit that allowed him to enjoy his leisure time fully. He was one of the happy few to possess a Ford Cabriolet. When he got married, however, he realized that being a shopkeeper did not fit his entrepreneurial temperament.

My father (second from right) in front of his shop.

After I was born, my father's determination prevailed and he decided to build a power plant. At that time, Wilno was already electrified, but not the surrounding villages. With my mother's support, he began searching in the Wilno region and eventually set his sights on Holszany, a small town of about 5,000 people, 70 kilometers southeast of Wilno. Holszany had no electricity. A river flowed nearby and was large enough to build a dam and create a three-meter-high waterfall, sufficient to run a turbine.

The surrounding lands belonged to an important landlord, called Yagmin. He was Russian and owned a castle on the top of the hill between Holszany and the place where my father intended to build his power plant. For the peasants who worked Yagmin's land, he was a true lord. As in the Middle Ages, they would take off their hats and kiss his hand.

The villagers and the inhabitants of the castle were still using kerosene lamps at the time. My father, who was not shy, went to meet Yagmin and presented his project to him in Russian. They

I am in the third row (fourth from left; there is a little cross on my hat).
The school director is standing in the middle of the last row.
Our teachers are Mrs. Samuelovna (left) and Mrs. Pavlovna (right).

negotiated for a bit and eventually signed a contract. The deal was done; Yagmin was the first to install electricity in his castle.

My father invested his entire energy and expertise into the construction of the power plant. He did it by himself, without the help of either engineers or architects. At the place of our future house, he built a shed where he stayed in the beginning. Next, he hired workers to build the dam. He then borrowed money from the bank, which allowed him to buy a turbine and a dynamo. Meanwhile, my mother and I stayed in Wilno with my grandparents. Every once in a while, whenever he had time, my father would come see us by bus or on horseback. He had sold both his car and his shop to finance his project.

I used to go to a Yiddish-language school, which was called after its director, Mrs. Shevelovitch-Katz. It was on Trocka Street, near where we lived.

It took my father less than three years to build the hydropower station. Our new home was outside the village, close to the plant,

1933. My mother and I walking down Mickiewicz Boulevard in Wilno.

and we had a telephone line, № 12. All that remained to do was to draw the electric lines over three kilometers and provide the local population with electrical meters. My mother worked alongside my father and managed accounting.

We used to have three dogs. The big German shepherd was tied with a rope that was long enough to make a full circle around the house. He was our guardian. The other two dogs were smaller and played around freely. The surrounding countryside was fertile with wheat, corn, and beets under cultivation, meadows, and forests.

More than a third of Holszany's population was Jewish. They all lived on relatively good terms with their Christian neighbors, despite an ever-present latent antisemitism. Jews were mostly merchants, craftsmen, and innkeepers, who took care of horse-drawn vehicles. Their material situation became significantly worse in 1925, however, when weekly markets with mostly Jewish owners were shut down. The markets were subsequently partially replaced by shops run by gentiles.

In 1935, we left Wilno to settle in our new home, a few kilometers away from Holszany, close to the power plant. I was eight years old and attending a private school in the synagogue, called *Tarbut*[1],

The Tarbut School in Holszany, c. 1935. I am in the top row
(fourth from left, a cross above my head).

[1] Tarbut—from Hebrew, "teaching"—indicates a group of Jewish schools in Poland where classes are taught in Hebrew.

which had five grades with a total of ninety pupils. In addition to subjects approved by the Ministry of Education, three languages were taught there: Hebrew, Yiddish, and Polish. Tuition was based on the parents' incomes. Still, the school suffered from a deficit, which is why it received donations from Holszany alumni who had emigrated to the USA.

The two 1937 photographs illustrate our life in Holszany.

In the boat: I, my mother, and Luba (my father's sister) behind her, my maternal grandfather, and my father.

My maternal grandfather, Kiva Badasz, used to produce cardboard boxes. He had set up his workshop on the ground floor of his house near Wilno University, on Slowacki Street. My grandmother, Fradl, cooked delicious meals. Often when I was staying with them, I would remove my trousers and hide in bed to avoid going home.

My paternal grandfather, Gerszon Malkes, was a bookbinder. He lived at 6 Ciasna Street in his three-story house close to the Lukiszki prison and Mickiewicz Boulevard.

*My parents and me
at ten years old
in Holszany.*

Like my grandparents, my parents were Zionists and not really religious. On major religious holidays, we would all gather to recite prayers in my maternal grandparents' house, where the atmosphere was more pleasant thanks to my uncle Grisza, who was a true *bon vivant*.

The Jerusalem of the North, as Napoleon called Vilna during his Russian campaign, or Yerusholayim di Lite in Yiddish, was the capital of Yiddishland[2] and an important city. Of its 200,000 citizens before the war, half were Polish, 35% were Jewish, and the remaining 15% Russians, Lithuanians, Belorussians, and Karaites.[3] There were many schools in the city that attracted students of Jewish theology as well as some of the most eminent rabbis. The heart of Wilno's old town was also the poorer Jewish quarter of the city. Street names there were in both Yiddish and Polish. Jews lived more or less separately from Poles. The two groups' occupations were therefore complementary: while Christians were most often clerks, soldiers, or peasants, Jews were merchants or craftsmen.

Cultural life in Wilno was very advanced. In both communities, there were numerous actors, musicians, writers, teachers, and

---

2 Literally, "Jewish world."

3 Karaite Jews are "Readers of the Hebrew Scriptures," yet were not persecuted by the Nazis.

doctors. The relationship between Jews and Poles, however, was strained. We did not mix, except to go on a strike together whenever a social conflict occurred. In Polish theaters, Polish plays were staged. In Jewish theaters, plays were in Yiddish and by Jewish authors.

The Jewish community was not monolithic. Rather, it was shaped by a variety of different ideas and ideologies. Thus, there were the followers of the religious Zionist organization Mizrachi; the right-wing Zionists represented by the Betar Movement; the Socialist-Zionists of Hashomer Hatzair, and the members of the General Jewish Labor Bund, the Jewish workers' union. Eminent people, such as the founder of Zionism, Theodor Herzl, and the pioneer of the more radical Zionism, the Revisionist Ze'ev Jabotinsky, came to Wilno to present their ideas to the population and to encourage the young generations to emigrate to Palestine.

Education was designed to fit the diversity of the Jewish community: about 90% of all students attended a dozen religious schools called yeshivot or secular schools and high schools where classes were taught in either Yiddish or Hebrew. Tarbut schools gave one the opportunity to earn a high school diploma, called matura. In ORT schools,[4] trades, handicrafts, and agricultural skills were taught in view of a possible departure to Palestine. Only about 10% of Jewish children attended Polish schools. Yiddish school textbooks and copies of the Bible in Hebrew were published by the two world-famous Wilno printers Kletskin and Romm.

Children from the surrounding villages often went to school in Wilno. With its more than a hundred synagogues[5] and many yeshivot, the Jewish town was characterized by intense and lively scientific, social, and cultural activity. Theatre performances and

---

[4] World ORT (Association for the Promotion of Skilled Trades) is a non-governmental training Jewish organization founded in 1880 in Saint-Petersburg.

[5] Of the hundred or so synagogues in the early 1930s, only one remains today.

concerts were regular events. The library on Straszun Street had more than 100,000 books in Hebrew and Yiddish. Furthermore, YIVO[6] was founded in Wilno in 1925 and published many good textbooks in Hebrew and Yiddish. The Yiddish spoken in Wilno was pure and literary and set a standard throughout the rest of the Jewish world.

In the 1930s, antisemitism in Poland became even more antagonistic with the death of Marshal Joseph Pilsudski.[7] The Polish nationalist party Endecja[8] stirred up hatred against Jewish people. Despite the fact that the government had condemned Endecja, a pogrom took place in Wilno in November 1931. Jews were attacked and shops and homes were set on fire. Many were injured and one was killed. Endecja supporters elevated a Polish nationalist to the status of a national hero. On the eve of the war, antisemitism had become especially strong among students. The university adopted a numerus clausus policy. The so-called "ghetto benches" were reserved for Jews. Many left to pursue their studies in Germany and France.

Antisemitism was fueled by the church and economic circumstances. Not a single day would go by without antisemitic caricatures appearing on the façades of churches. Everyone was forced to take off their hat when passing underneath the Virgin's icon at the Ostra Brama city-gate. Since they were frequently attacked there, most Jews preferred to take a detour and avoid the area. For Orthodox Jews, who were easily recognizable by their clothing, it was better not to be seen in that part of the city at all.

---

[6] YIVO or Yiddish Scientific Institute, also known as YIVO Institute for Jewish Research, New York.

[7] Marshal Joseph Pilsudski was leader of the Second Polish Republic (1926-1935) and was in favor of recognizing Poland's numerous ethnic and religious groups. He died of liver cancer on May 12, 1935.

[8] *Narodowa Demokracja* in Polish. *Endecja* is a name derived from the abbreviation ND.

It should be noted that Poland's population in the 1930s was 33 million, of which 3.5 million were Jews—that is, more than 10%. Four hundred thousand Jews lived in the capital, Warsaw. At that time there were some 150,000 Jews in England, 300,000 in France, and 500,000 in Germany, where the population in each of the three countries was nearly twice as big as Poland's. Jews thus represented less than one percent of total population in each of the three countries.

The disproportion of the Jewish population between western and eastern countries goes back to the Edit of Expulsion signed by the Spanish Inquisition in 1492. As they were expelled from the west, Jews were invited by Polish kings to contribute to the country's economic development.

With time, Jews settled not only in cities, but also in villages where in some cases they represented more than half of the local population. After a while, living with Christians deteriorated, forcing Jew to emigrate to Palestine, the United States, and even Latin America in the 1920s and 1930s.

During the Soviet occupation in 1939-41, a number of Jews were exiled to Siberia; others fled the Nazis to the Soviet Union. The Nazi occupation in 1941-1944 virtually exterminated the entire Jewish population in Eastern Europe with the exception of Bulgaria where Jews were protected.

After the end of the war, in 1945, the exodus reversed, continued towards the west. Many who had been liberated from concentration camps or deportation in Siberia settled in the United States or Palestine, thus allowing the creation of the State of Israel in 1948.

I do not think we left Wilno and settled in Holszany because of antisemitism or the 1931 pogrom. We became accustomed to everything. The main reason was certainly my father's entrepreneurship, encouraged by my mother and his cousins, the wealthy Riwkes brothers.

*My grandfather Kiva
sitting in front of
our house in Holszany
with Lalka at his feet.*

The power plant was a success and even surpassed my father's expectations as most villagers signed up. However, there was still a surplus of power, especially during the day. My father thought about it and noticed that shoemakers used wooden molds to make shoes and boots. At the time, there were no shoe factories in Poland, except the Czech firm *Bata*. Everyone ordered their shoes at the shoemaker's. My father realized that he could use the extra power and the abundance of wood in the surrounding forests to build a factory for wooden shoe molds. The idea caught on. He bought the necessary machinery and built the factory right next to the power plant. My father thus began making molds in addition to producing electricity. He was a rich man, or at least so it seemed on the outside, but in reality he also had significant debts after having borrowed money to finance his projects.

In 1937, he opened another shoe mold factory in Wilno.

All was going well for us. My parents were happy and I was a well-behaved and pampered only child. I was *Shleimele*, my mother's only son, the apple of her eye. She took me to school in the village and came to pick me up every afternoon with a snack. To me, my mother was a saint: the expression *yiddishe mame* fit her well. She devoted herself heart and soul to her husband and family. I had a few friends but they lived in the village and I saw them only at school.

My grandfather Kiva sitting on a pile of chipped wood in Holszany.

My mother had a sister, Mania, and three brothers. The oldest, Yuli, wished to study medicine but was denied access to Wilno University due to admission quotas. He therefore went to study in Moscow in 1917 (before the Bolshevik Revolution). As soon as he got his diploma, he got married and settled down there.

The youngest brother, Boris, did not see his future in Wilno. He emigrated to Brussels long before the war and, having learned his father's craft, opened his own cardboard factory there. Yuli and Boris had both already left Wilno before I was born, so I met them only after the war. My mother's middle brother, Grisza, had gone to Belgium a few years after Boris and worked there with him.

After Grisza's departure, my maternal grandparents, who were elderly, decided to sell their house and the cardboard factory, leave Wilno, and join their two sons in Brussels. Aunt Mania married

A firm postcard of the shoe mold factory.

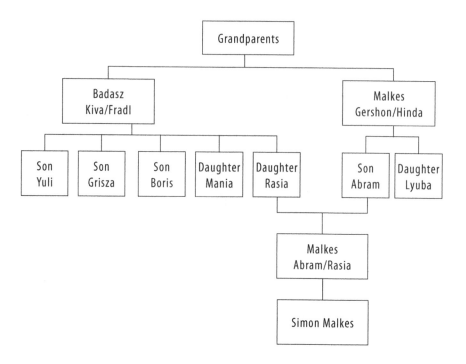

a man called Samuel Wojczyk. They had a son, Maurice, and lived in Rovno, a town about 400 kilometers south of Wilno, where Samuel worked as an accountant in the family brewery.

My father had a beautiful sister called Luba. She married Max Lapidus, with whom she had two daughters.

Such was my and my family's life before the Molotov-Ribbentrop Pact, before the war, the Soviet occupation, and Jews' extermination by the Nazis.

***

In 1991, many years after the end of the war and the death of both Stalin and Hitler, I went back to my hometown Wilno, now Vilnius, with my partner, Denise, whose father had likewise been born there. At first, Vilnius seemed unrecognizable and empty. Street names and house numbers had been changed and the city's 65,000 Jews had all disappeared. The colorful and lively melting pot of my childhood memories was gone. One could have counted Wilno Jews on the fingers of one's hand; the rest came for the most part from the Soviet Union. In order to meet Jews, one had to go to the Friday night service that was held in the city's only remaining synagogue. It was then that I met, among others, Fania Brancowskaja, bornée Yocheles, whose father used to be friends with mine and exercised the same profession.

Denise and I went to see my grandfather's building at 6 Ciasna Street, which had become 8 Ankstoji Street. A couple of residents came down to meet me where I was standing. They asked me in Russian why I was interested in their building. "Was I the owner and had I come to recover my property?" they inquired, anxious for their future. I replied that indeed the building had once belonged to my grandfather who had been killed.

We then went to see the house where Denise's father's family, the Milezkowski's, had lived. Her mother had left Odessa and moved to France when she was four or five years old. It was the first time that Denise ever saw the house. She immediately understood why her father had left Wilno. What a contrast with his current life in France. His emigration had been driven by economic reasons. My mother's parents' house on Slowacki Street, which they had sold before the war in order to go to Brussels, has become the site of a Lithuanian institution.

I shall never forget my visit to the Lithuanian Embassy in Paris in 1991, soon after the country had obtained its independence. I met the ambassador and asked him how to get back my grandfather's house in Vilnius. "If we gave you back everything," he replied bluntly, "what would be there left to us?" I was shocked, got up and left.

Two years later, in 1993, I went back to Lithuania and met the Shapiro family, who had come from the former Soviet Union and wished to go to the United States. I told Mr. Shapiro that, before the war, my father had had a power plant in Holszany, in today's Belarus. Mr. Shapiro then suggested taking me there by car. It was less than an hour's drive away, yet I was not sure whether I could cross the border without a visa. "You westerners are so naïve," Mr. Shapiro laughed, "give the customs officer a few dollars and he will be happy." He was right: we thus managed to cross the border without any difficulty.

When we arrived in Holszany, we first passed Yagmin's castle, which was in ruins. We continued on and to my surprise, we then saw that the power plant and our house had disappeared without a trace, as if they had never existed. Farther on, we reached the river of my childhood. It had almost dried up. In less than sixty years, my father's business had been reduced to nothing. I then understood that we had no future there. The east of all our misfortunes and pain had led us to a much better place to live, France.

Chapter Two

The War: The Soviet Occupation (1939-1941)

The German army attacked Poland less than a fortnight after the signing of the Nazi-Soviet non-aggression pact on August 23, 1939. Also known as the Molotov-Ribbentrop agreement, the pact stipulated the division of Poland into two spheres of influence. The Nazis called their attack *Drang nach Osten*, "drive toward the east." The imbalance of forces was striking: Polish cavalry could not compete with German aviation and tanks.

In September 1939, while the conflict was still not over, the Soviet army entered Eastern Poland in keeping with the borderline, agreed upon by the belligerents. Slowly but steadily and without bloodshed, the Soviets fulfilled their Machiavellian plan. They split Eastern Poland into three parts. The northern part with Wilno (future Vilnius) was given to Lithuania; the central bit with Holszany, to Belarus; and Ukraine got the south with Rovno, the town where my mother's sister lived. The latter two were thus annexed to the already Soviet republics bureaucracy and the

*During the war the Western part of Poland (pink on this map) was occupied
by the Nazis, the small North-Eastern part (also shown in pink) was given
by the Soviets to Lithuania, the area colored green on the map—to Belarus,
and the South-East (colored in yellow)—to Ukraine.*

NKVD[9] were active. The Soviet army put pressure on Lithuania
to impose a procommunist government with a prime minister
of its own choice, Justas Paleckis. Meanwhile, Moscow applied
similar pressure on the remaining two Baltic countries, Latvia
and Estonia.

With a few changes in cabinet and armed with patient
persistence, the Soviets were to annex all three countries by June
1940. The transfer of the Lithuanian capital from Kaunas to Vilnius,
however, did not go as smoothly. The Polish majority rose against
Jews and Lithuanians to the extent that the Soviet army had to be
called upon for help. Calm was then slowly restored.

---

[9]   NKVD or People's Commissariat for Internal Affairs was a Soviet law enforcement
     agency. Founded in 1934, it was associated with the Soviet secret police.

Left-wing supporters and Jews, who had been victims of antisemitism, became involved in the Soviet administration in a spirit of revenge and hopes for a better life. In contrast, supporters of all other political movements and entrepreneurs were treated severely.

My father had come to Vilnius to oversee work at his shoe mold factory. All was going well. He then visited his cousins the Riwkes. There were three Riwkes cousins: two brothers, of whom one was blind, and a widowed sister with a child. They were very rich and traded in bicycles and bicycle parts.

The Riwkes and my father talked about the new situation and the future of their respective businesses. They knew perfectly well what the Soviets' attitude towards the wealthy people was. The Riwkes, who had 20 kilograms of gold coins and 100-carat diamonds, had decided to hide their fortune and asked my agile father for help. They buried the bag of gold in the basement and inserted the diamonds in a hole of a wooden cupboard. Once sealed, the hiding spot became invisible.

I remember how, as a child, I used to visit the Riwkes with my mother. The blind brother Uriasz used to call me *Salamoshke*. He would open the safe and let me play with the gold coins in the bag.

My father took care of his business, helped his cousins, and then returned to Holszany. The NKVD came soon after that to arrest him. He was accused of being a capitalist and exploiter of the working class and was sent to prison. My mother was given 48 hours to leave the house. Brave as she was, she packed as many belongings as she could and rented a carriage, with which we left for Vilnius. Holszany was already part of Belarus where the Stalinist machine had been set in motion sooner than in Lithuania.

As soon as he heard of the Soviets' arrival, Yagmin, the wealthy landowner where my father's power plant was, fled, fearing imprisonment or deportation to Siberia. These were the only two options that capitalists (whether real or imagined) had under the Stalinist regime.

Soon after Lithuania became a Soviet republic, all four members of the Riwkes family were deported to Siberia. The NKVD's strange way of functioning can hardly remain unnoticed. My father had employed more than twenty people and had lots of debts, whereas the Riwkes had only a couple of employees. How could one explain such a difference in treatment? The Riwkes had probably been denounced for their fortune. After the war, we all cherished their luck to have been deported to Siberia. They would have never survived the Holocaust.

The purge organized by the Soviets did not affect only the rich. Thousands of Polish officers were deported and executed in the Katyn massacre. Intellectuals and right-wing leaders, Jews and non-Jews, likewise faced deportation. Factories, principal buildings, such as my grandfather's, and all important firms were nationalized. Still, they let my grandfather stay in his apartment. Landlords' lands were divided and redistributed among peasants.

Even though antisemitism from the Polish era had certainly disappeared, Soviet passports still indicated "Jew" under nationality. Jews did not attend the synagogue as openly as before (nor did Catholics go to church either). *Yeshivot* were still there, however, and ritual slaughter was not prohibited despite communists' violently antireligious ideology.

Some people, Jews and non-Jews alike, were satisfied with the new regime. Jews were pleased because they were not victims of antisemitic persecutions anymore. As for the poor, they expected an illusory hope of obtaining the wealth of the rich.

In Vilnius, my mother rented an apartment on 6 Rudnicka Street where the Jewish school, the *Real Gymnasium*, was. Later that same street became part of the ghetto. My mother engaged in small trade that allowed us to survive: she bought articles from one person and sold them to another, making a little profit as an intermediary. We thus managed to get by.

My father was still in prison. He was let out with all the other prisoners when the Germans arrived. His cousins the Riwkes were perishing in Siberia. I was nearly thirteen years old, the age of *Bar Mitzvah*, but I do not recall having celebrated the event. Our priorities were different. Hundreds of Jews were coming from Polish territories under German occupation and were bringing us very sad news. Still, the worst was yet to come.

Later we saw that the deported survived as opposed to those who remained and perished.

Chapter Three
The War: The German Occupation (1941-1944)

On June 22, 1941, the Germans surprisingly attacked the Soviet Union, in spite of the non-aggression pact they had signed less than two years earlier. The Blitzkrieg meant that the German Army was rapidly advancing on all fronts. The Red Army's confusion was complete: soldiers tried to flee to the east and many were imprisoned.

The situation in the Jewish community was similar, although the majority of people did not move. The young in particular tried reaching Russia. Some of them succeeded, yet others got caught up by the Germans' swift progress and had to return.

My father had not yet been liberated, so we decided to stay in Vilnius. My mother's sister and her family, the Wojczyks, left Rovno for Russia. We found out that they had succeeded many years after the liberation. A couple of days after the war began, the Germans entered Vilnius. All Soviet prisoners were liberated and my father returned home. I could hardly recognize him: he was so thin his pants had to be tied up with a string.

Lithuanians welcomed their liberators with enthusiasm despite the fact that the Russians had given them the north of Poland. A great number of Lithuanians joined the SS and the German army. The Gestapo settled in Vilnius and the Einsatzgruppen[10] very soon began killing Jews with the help of their Lithuanian collaborators. Posters in both German and Lithuanian forbade Jews to use public transportation. Jews could no longer circulate in the main streets of the city or walk on the sidewalks. They had to wear yellow Stars of David on their chests and backs.

The Gestapo insisted upon the formation of a Judenrat,[11] led by Saul Trocki. Its first mission was to collect a tax of one million Reichsmarks in gold and precious objects. The result, however, did not meet the Germans' expectations and Judenrat members who had brought the objects were arrested and taken to an unknown place, from which they never returned.

Lithuanian *chapunes* (literally "catchers" in Yiddish) were in charge of kidnapping Jews in the streets and even at their homes and taking them to the Lukiszki prison close to my grandparents' house. They received 10 Reichsmarks per Jew. When the prison was full, men, women, and children were taken in a truck, sometimes by foot even, to Ponary forest 10 kilometers away from Vilnius. The Russians had dug enormous pits in the oak and birch forest with the intention of storing fuel tanks. The pits were instead filled with the bodies of Jews who were shot dead.

In about three months, more than 25,000 Jews were shot in Ponary by the German and Lithuanian *Einsatzgruppen.* The infernal machine never stopped. My paternal grandparents, their daughter Luba, her husband Max Lapidus, and their two daughters—the

---

[10] *Einsatzgruppen* were SS death squads of the Third Reich that were in charge of mass killings of Jews and opponents to the regime.

[11] The *Judenrat* was an administrative body representing Jews during the German occupation.

elder's name was Sofia; I forget the younger one's name—were executed even before the ghetto was set up.

Early September 1941, posters announcing the assassination of two Germans by Jews appeared in the city. *Gebietskomissar* Hans Hingst and his SS assistants for Jewish Affairs, Kittel and Weiss, declared that measures had to be taken to protect Germans. The ghetto's boundaries in the city center were designated by the Gestapo and the Lithuanian militia. A week later, all remaining Jews were penned up in the two newly-established ghettos: nearly 30,000 in the large ghetto and about 10,000 in the smaller one. Both ghettos were surrounded by walls topped by barbed wire to isolate them from the exterior world. All windows looking out of the ghetto were walled up.

So far we had managed to slip through the net. We did not have to move since our apartment on 6 Rudnicka Street was inside the large ghetto. We did not stay there alone, however: four more people were housed with us.

The *Judenrat* and the Jewish police settled in our building (where the Jewish school used to be) and were supposed to maintain order and assist the Germans with their dirty jobs. Jacob Gens was the *Judenrat*'s leader and head of the Jewish police. Gens was a former Lithuanian officer, whose non-Jewish wife had remained outside of the ghetto.

The *Judenrat* had to provide a comprehensive account of every ghetto resident's name, age, and profession. The Germans could thus use manpower to their advantage, rather than feed Jews for nothing. We could sometimes choose our workplace according to our profession, or it was imposed upon us. We received an *Ausweis* (work card; *Schein* in Yiddish) whose color varied according to criteria established by the Germans. The *Judenrat* also gave an *Ausweis* of the right color to those who worked for the ghetto administration, the police, and the medical service, in addition to artists and intellectuals.

My father, our friends the Kloks and the Greisdorfs (also electricians), and I were registered to work at *Heereskraftfahrpark* (HKP) workshops for the repairing of military vehicles. Some Jews worked at the Gestapo as handymen and were suspected to be traitors. Rumor had it that they were providing the Germans with information. Some people would go that far to save their lives. Naturally, we never learned the truth.

Every morning, workers gathered at the ghetto gates and were split into groups according to their workplace. We were led by a supervisor in charge of maintaining order and walked in columns down the city streets. Sometimes, a German soldier accompanied us.

Two months after the two ghettos were set up, the Germans decided to get rid of the small ghetto. Everyone with the exception of a minority, who had an *Ausweis* of the right color, was taken to Ponary. The Jewish police assisted the Germans during the roundup and for some of us Jacob Gens was considered a traitor. Others thought he did all that he could to save as many lives as possible. We all felt disgusted and sad and asked ourselves when it would be our turn. But time heals all wounds and our desire to live was so strong.

There were seven of us now in the apartment where we used to be three before the ghetto was established. At night, rooms became dormitories; during the day we would pile up the mattresses to free some space. I recall a young and good-looking policeman who lived in our house with his parents. His fiancée was a splendid girl who likewise lived in the ghetto. Shortly before the ghetto's liquidation, they decided to flee and join the partisans. Alas, they got caught in the city and were taken to the Gestapo, where they were tortured and had their eyes gouged out. We were told about their destiny by the Jews who were working at the Gestapo. The drama that took place in our apartment when the young man's parents found out is beyond words.

September 1941.
It is my fourteenth birthday and I live in a ghetto.

Another man that shared our apartment was an elderly bachelor and chess champion who taught me how to play. I was fourteen years old and tall, but at the sight of the SS always lowered my head and fled like everyone else. We felt like we were rats for being Jews. If a member of the SS did not like you, he could shoot you down as easily as they crushed a fly. Whenever one of us fell on the ground, he was beaten and trod upon. This might be well-known today, but it will always be hard for me talk about it.

Those who think that life in the ghetto was disorganized do not know Jews and Germans well. I now realize that the genuine social life that took place there was a form of resistance for the adults who tried in every possible way not to lose their foothold. Children went to school and learned how to read. Rachel Margolis worked at the library on 6 Straszun Street, where intellectuals met secretly to organize the resistance and not let themselves be slaughtered like sheep. The first to join the resistance bought weapons and practiced shooting. Actors rehearsed Jewish plays in Yiddish and Hebrew; musicians gave concerts to which Jacob Gens sometimes invited members of the Gestapo and the SS. Musical competitions were organized and allowed winners to make ends meet.

One might think that the ceaseless executions had completely eradicated Jewish talent from the ghetto, yet many found a way of artistically expressing themselves, thus leaving a testimony for posterity. Some recorded ghetto events in the form of a chronicle, while others, like Avrom Sutzkewer, wrote poems. Then there were those like Shmerke Kaczerginski, who composed songs.[12]

Herman Kruk and other senior YIVO scholars dedicated themselves entirely to preserving the library's and the Institute for Jewish Research's precious collections by secretly taking books out of the ghetto in order to hide them somewhere safe. Intellectuals were assisted in their task by Anna Simaite, a Lithuanian lady who received the title Righteous Among the Nations after the war. Thanks to her, many books and documents have been saved.

Herman Kruk kept the ghetto's chronicle every day. I thought this a pointless and time-wasting activity at the time, as we were

[12] My friend Maria Krupoves, an extremely talented Polish singer who sings in Yiddish without the slightest accent, recorded songs composed in the ghetto, such as "Never Say You Are Walking Down Your Last Road." It is easy to guess where this road leads.

My father's yellow Ausweis, which I managed to keep.
It was worth a fortune in the ghetto.

all doomed. When the ghetto was liquidated, he was unfortunately deported to Estonia, where he died. His diary was published in Yiddish by the YIVO in New York in 1961.

Although a number of physicians from the medical corps were executed before the ghetto was set up, those who managed to survive, such as Schabad-Gawronska, Libo, Sedlis, and Dworzecki, to name a few, strived harder than ever to maintain the hospital and the orphanage that looked after children whose parents had been executed. Hygiene was taken very seriously in order to avoid an epidemic, which would have pushed the Germans to set the entire ghetto on fire.

Chimney sweeps and undertakers played a special role since they were able to leave the ghetto. Chimney sweeps could enter and exit houses by the roofs and could also sell goods and buy provisions, while undertakers could leave the ghetto in order to bury the dead in the cemetery outside of town. Sometimes undertakers helped a child or an adult escape and hide on the Aryan side. Moreover, it was easier for them to sneak in food since they were rarely checked.

In the meantime, Aktions or massive killings never stopped. In March 1942, the Germans required that we hand in the elderly and all who did not have an Ausweis of the right color. With the help of the Jewish police, the SS rounded up and murdered more than 5,000 people. The ghetto plunged into deep despair; panic was omnipresent. The ones with an unacceptable Ausweis either hid themselves or paid for their name to be added as husband, wife, or child by those who did possess the savior document.[13]

I have often been asked to describe our everyday life in the ghetto. It generally revolved around food and survival. Those who could afford it found enough food to survive. The more deprived remained in the ghetto and died of starvation and exhaustion in the streets. We were privileged to be HKP workers and got a bit of soup for lunch every day. My mother, who had remained in the ghetto, managed to prepare thin soup for dinner. There were seven of us at dinner and we all looked to see what the others had on their plates.

There were 18,000 people left in the ghetto in the spring of 1942. Between March 1942 and the summer of 1943, the Germans needed manpower and stopped organizing *Aktions*.

---

[13] Rachel Klok had thus taken as "husband" a friend who did not have the right *Ausweis*. When I was looking through the lists of HKP workers many years later, I found out that our *Ausweis* mentioned the name of a certain Fania. My father is not there anymore to tell me more about it.

We were employed at the HKP virtually since the ghetto's creation. The conditions were acceptable. Jews were not mistreated and we were never beaten. Unlike other workplaces, we had the right to rest for an hour at noon. Food was scarce, but there was always some left to take home. The six HKP workshops specialized in different areas and were scattered around the cityubder the command of Major Karl Plagge. 250 German officers and soldiers worked there and supervised the Polish workers, Russian prisoners, and 500 Jews. Plagge was apparently the one who ordered his subordinates to treat his workers decently.

My father and I worked in the electrical workshop along with our friends the Kloks, their daughter Rachel, and the two Greisdorf brothers. Our fathers trained me and Rachel. Rachel was rewinding dynamos, while I specialized in electrical wiring of tracks. Two Wehrmacht soldiers, Gammer and Novak, were in charge of our workshop. They were unskilled and contented themselves with making sure workers kept busy.

After nearly a year of relative calm, the Gestapo found out that Yitzhak Wittenberg was the head of the FPO[14] and threatened to dispose of the entire ghetto if Gens did not hand him in. The news spread like wildfire. Wittenberg decided to surrender and swallowed a cyanide pill before the interrogation. He was succeeded by Abba Kowner, who survived and went to Israel after the war along with other members of the FPO, such as Rachel Margolis and Yitzhak Arad. The latter became general in the Israeli army, then president of Yad Vashem after retiring from the army. Abba Kowner dedicated himself to remembrance.

Following the Wittenberg incident and with their impending plan to liquidate the ghetto in mind, the SS enclosed Porubanek airport near Vilnius and rounded up 1,000 young and strong

---

[14]   FPO stands for *Fareynikte Partizaner Organizatsye* in Yiddish and is the name of the Jewish resistance organization.

Jews that were considered a threat. Their fate was decided in Ponary.

By September 1943, we had been working at the HKP for nearly two years. We knew that the German army was suffering defeat after defeat on the eastern front and that, thanks to the Americans who provided the Soviet army with arms, trucks, and food, German soldiers were retreating.

Around mid-September 1943, the head of the *Judenrat* and the Jewish police Jacob Gens was summoned by the Gestapo and never returned. We found out that he had been executed on the spot, but naturally we never learned why. His non-Jewish wife emigrated to the United States after the war.

All of the above events foreshadowed the ghetto's imminent liquidation. Inhabitants were overcome with panic and wondered what to do. Flee or hide? Where and for how long?

Major Plagge had also heard about the ghetto's fate. Two weeks before the liquidation, Kailis and HKP Jewish workers and their families were transferred to two different parts of the city outside of the ghetto. At the Kailis factory, several hundred Jews produced fur coats for the German army.

Many years after the war, much information about Major Karl Plagge was found by a small group of German researchers. We learned that, as soon as the liquidation of the ghetto was planned, Plagge went to Latvia's capital, Riga, to meet with the SS officer in charge of camps at the time. Plagge explained that the HKP needed its Jewish specialists. He was allowed to keep his Jewish workers and their families (a total of 1,200 people) and was given two large buildings at 37 Subocz Street where everyone was housed. Long before the war the two blocks were built by the Jewish philanthropist Baron de Hirsch to house poor Jews.

After the war, I heard that the Jews that had worked for the Gestapo had apparently also been settled like us outside the ghetto. I don't know if this is true, or if any survived.

On September 23, 1943, the ghetto's liquidation was officially announced by the Germans, who specified that Jews could choose to go to work in either Estonia or Latvia. Everyone took it for a trap and thought of Ponary. But what could they do? What alternative did they have? Was a *maline* (hiding place in Yiddish) really a solution? How much time could one stay hidden? And what was one supposed to do afterwards? Those who had some money left tried to join the HKP or Kailis workshops at all costs in order to stay in town. Only the few whose names had been added by the holders of an *Ausweis* from the HKP or Kailis could make it.

While the ghetto was surrounded by German, Ukrainian, and Lithuanian SS officers, a hundred young FPO members managed to escape in groups through the sewer at night and joined the partisans in the surrounding forests. Many survived, including my parents' friend's daughter Fania Brancowskaja, née Yocheles, who currently lives in Vilnius, the poet Avrom Sutzkewer, the compositor Shmerke Kaczerginski, and Yitzhak Arad.[15]

For once, Germans kept their word and about 15,000 Jews were taken from the ghetto to Rossa monastery in the outskirts of the city where a selection was carried out. Those capable of working were sent to Kaizerwald (Latvia), Klooge (Estonia), and other peat extraction camps; the rest were executed. Germans used charcoal extracted by slave laborers as fuel.

One hundred thousand people thus rest in Ponary. They are mostly Jews from Wilno and the surrounding region, but also foreign Jews and Soviet prisoners.

We learned more about the ghetto's liquidation from the few who remained hidden in the ghetto or who had fled Rossa during the night and had come to the HKP camp. There were only the 2,200 HKP and Kailis Jews left in Vilnius, but who knew for how much

---

[15] Avrom Sutzkever died in Israel in 2011. Shmerke Kaczerginski perished in an airplane accident in the Argentinean Andes in 1954.

longer? Both the HKP and Kailis camps were under the command of the Austrian SS officer Richter. He was a murderer and we gave him a nickname, Golosheika (Polish for "long exposed neck").

***

Long after the end of the war, I learned that, as the Soviet army was approaching the Baltic region in 1944, the Nazis had exterminated a great number of Jews and Russian prisoners in the Estonian camps. A small part of the inmates were evacuated to Dantzig. Some Jews from Kaizerwald were transferred to the camp in Stutthof, then to Magdebourg near Buchenwald. Such was my friend Asia Turgel's case: she was about to be evacuated from Polte-Magdebourg and sent on a death march when she escaped. She lives in Paris today.

Long before Vilna Jews, Fruma Hazanovsky from Holszany was also sent to Kaizerwald, Latvia to extract peat. When the Soviet army came closer, she was sent to Stutthof and later freed by the Russo-Polish army. A Polish officer recognized her: "Fruma, do you remember me? We went to school together!" Fruma is now 87 years old and lives in Israel. I went to visit her in 2012. Her epic story took three hours to tell and made my stomach cramp.

My childhood friend from Wilno, Meier Shapiro, lives in the United States today. I visited him as well in 2012. His story is different: when the ghetto was liquidated, he hid with his parents and sister in a *maline*, but they were quickly discovered. The SS split them, women and men apart, and put them on separate animal cars. Meier managed to jump off the train that night and wandered for some time until he got to Kailis. His stay in Kailis was not without difficulty. He was then sent to Kaizerwald, Latvia, then to Stutthof, and finally to a factory in Germany. When the Red Army liberated him, he had lost a lot of weight and all his strength; military physicians took care of him. Having regained his strength, he returned to Vilnius where he found his mother and his sister, four years younger, but alas not his father. Later, we met again in Lodz, Poland.

Many years after the war, in 2000, Lithuanian authorities questioned Fania Brancowskaja about resistance fighters who had avenged themselves on a village near Vilnius. They had issued an extradition request via Interpol for Arad and Margolis. The case produced a huge scandal around the world as several resistance groups, both Jewish and non-Jewish, had operated in the region. Lithuanian authorities eventually dropped the proceedings.

Chapter Four
The HKP
(1943-1944)

A fortnight before the ghetto's liquidation, all HKP workers and their families were transferred in military trucks to two blocks designated for us on Subocz Street. Each family got its own room, so we were not as crowded as we used to be in the ghetto. HKP workshops were reorganized. Some, such as the electrical, locksmithing, and carpentry workshops, were moved to 37 Subocz Street; others, such as the saddlery and the mechanical workshops, remained where they were. We, electricians, were privileged since our workshop was on the ground floor of our block. Our workshop foremen Gammer and Novak, with whom we had a good relationship, kept managing it. Those who worked elsewhere, outside of the HKP camp, walked in columns to their workplace every morning and returned in the evening.

We heard about the ghetto's liquidation from the rare survivors that hid inside the ghetto and then infiltrated the HKP camp at night. They were welcomed and given a room and work. Thanks to the good relationship we had with Werhmacht soldiers, everything was much simpler here, at the HKP camp, than it was in the ghetto. We were

The Kloks

not in contact with the Kailis Jews, but they probably received a few ghetto survivors as well.

There were panels around the city that indicated the HKP workshops' new locations. German soldiers who needed electrical repairs for their military trucks thus knew they had to come to 37 Subocz Street. Gammer received the soldiers and filled in the repair forms, often in my presence. If a dynamo or a starter broke down, I was the one to remove and bring them to the workshop. If I was not there, Gammer would look for me: "Wo ist der kleine Malkes?" (Where is the young Malkes?). I worked mainly on cars' electrical wiring outside, whereas my father and the others worked mostly inside the workshop. Without any false modesty, my German improved quite a bit since I had been working at the HKP. When I found myself one on one with a soldier, he would often ask me not to hurry and to take my time repairing his vehicle. The message was clear: he wanted to delay his departure for the eastern front. Depending on the problem, I would tell him to come back in a week or two and bring me some food. Occasionally, I would even sabotage the vehicle by creating a new failure. I thus helped the soldier, the Soviet Army, and myself.

When the truck was fixed and if the soldier was nice, I would sometimes ask him to take me for a test drive downtown. They rarely refused. If they agreed, I would take off my yellow star and we would pass by the market where I would buy supplies, then return to the camp. It was a win-win situation: I was pleased and the soldier got to spend a few days less at the front. Such sort of transaction would have been impossible in the ghetto. Here, on Subocz Street, it was possible to leave the camp by car with a soldier.

I never had any problems with the Wehrmacht officers. One day a soldier saw my yellow patch and asked me: "Are you really Jewish? That's strange as you don't have a hooked nose!"

Sometimes I sold rings to officers. Rachel Klok's friend, whose name she had added on her *Ausweis*, was a jeweler. He made silver rings upon request; he used to set them with a slab of black stone and a gold monogram on top. Naturally, I did not suggest such a deal to all soldiers. I chose them in terms of appearance, rank, and accent. Never did a soldier refuse to pay me or treat me condescendingly because I was Jewish. I was paid either in cash or supplies, or both. Everyone was satisfied and we were not hungry anymore. I could even resell food at times. The transactions were quite enjoyable, even though my father often scolded me. Still, I was very careful.

It was 1944, the Russians were standing up to the Germans and were advancing towards the west. We knew that we were going to be annihilated before the Russians reached Vilnius. Upon our arrival on Subocz Street in September 1943, my father began building a *maline* (hideout) with a few friends. There was a cellar underneath a bread oven in our block. They walled up the cellar's entrance and built a new one underneath the bread oven, which could be moved on virtually invisible rails. The construction took place at night, after work. It was a safe hideout. Others, such as

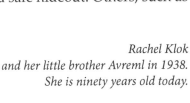
Rachel Klok
and her little brother Avreml in 1938.
She is ninety years old today.

The Greisdorfs

the Kloks and the Greisdorfs, for instance, who were related, set up a shared hiding place under the roof.

The HKP was no paradise in spite of my little business. One day we were summoned in the blocks' courtyard and the sadistic SS officer Richter, whom we called Golosheika, and his henchmen brought down the Zalkinds. The couple had tried fleeing the HKP camp, but got caught in town. They were hanged in front of everybody as an example to us. The rope snapped under Zalkind's weight and he fell on the ground. Rather than free the hanged, as one would normally do—nothing was normal there—Richter took out his gun and without the slightest hesitation shot him in the head. Everyone was shocked. My father was particularly upset and despite the *maline,* he asked a Pole to take us in. We entrusted him with our belongings and some valuables. As soon as he had it all, the Pole forgot about us. There was nothing we could do but weep.

Another even more dramatic event took place in March 1944. Richter and his henchmen came again, this time with a truck of reinforcements at the gate. He ordered all women with children under ten to come down. Some probably thought that there was nothing to fear since their children were only infants. Luckily, not all women came down with their children; some hid them. Children were first separated from their mothers and then ghastly and unheard of things happened. Children were screaming and crying, mothers were struggling with the guards to tear their children away from them, others wanted to get on the truck with them, but were violently pushed back. The truck quickly left with about 200 children on board. Desolation grew when men returned from work that evening. Fortunately, Klok's and Greisdorf's sons, who were both ten, had been hidden. They survived and live in Canada today. I shall talk about the Greisdorfs' and young Lazar's role in more detail in the last chapter.

The *Kinder Aktion* (Children Operation) left us in a state of utter shock and desolation and also foretold our future. It happened during Plagge's absence. We could feel his profound sorrow when he found out about it upon his return. Could he have prevented them from doing it? We doubted it: our true masters were the SS. We were merely rented to the Wehrmacht, which paid them a certain amount of money for each Jewish slave. The same *Aktion* was carried out at Kailis as well.

For Plagge, it was a warning sign that the same *Aktion* could happen again, this time with women. So he went to either Germany or Belgium to contact Reitz and Herbert Meier's firm *Kleiderreparatur*, which produced and repaired German military uniforms. He negotiated the manufacture's subcontracting and that uniforms be repaired by HKP women. Sewing-machines were set up in one of our blocks. Had he asked for his superiors' permission to negotiate with Reitz and Herbert Meier? We will never know. Plagge thus wanted to protect women from future danger.

In April 1944, about three months before liberation, my mother fell seriously sick and had to have an operation. My father told

Gammer and Plagge about it. Major Plagge and his faithful driver took the risk of driving her to the town hospital. She was taken care of and remained there until liberation. As it will become clear very soon, the entire family was lucky she did not stay with us.

The Russians were advancing steadily. In early July 1944, Major Plagge gathered us all and announced that the HKP was about to close its workshops and be moved to the West. He told us that he was, unfortunately, unable to take us with him, but that the SS knew how to take good care of forced laborers. The message was perfectly clear; we knew what was going to happen and what we had to do.

That night some twenty or so youths, who probably did not have a hideout, cut the lattice of the locksmith workshop's windows, jumped from the first floor, and went off freely. Bill Begell was one of them. He survived and emigrated to the United States. I met him in Jerusalem in 2005. As to my father and I, we went down to our *maline*. When we arrived, we found out that the group had more than doubled in size at the last moment: we were 37 instead of 15. It is impossible to negotiate in the face of death; everyone wants to save their life. We pushed the oven aside, quickly went downstairs, and closed it behind us before someone else came. We all asked ourselves how much time we had to remain in there.

The following morning we heard boots and shouting: *"Alles raus!"* (Everyone get out!). We understood that the SS and the Lithuanians were there. We could hear them, yet we could not see anything. The Kloks, who had front-row seats and saw everything from their hideout underneath the roof, later told us what had happened. Anyone who did not have a hideout was taken down to the courtyard and from there to the well-known destination of Ponary.

The Germans' count did not come out right, however, so they guessed that there were Jews hiding somewhere. The hunt began and some hideouts were found out. We understood that when we heard the SS shouting: they were yelling, not just talking loudly.

The two HKP blocks. The headstone is in memory of the Jews discovered in their malines and murdered on the spot.

They used choking gas to uncover suspected hideouts. Unfortunate people quickly came out with their hands in the air. Everyone was shot on the spot, in the courtyard between the two blocks. We heard gunfire, not knowing what was going on. The shots ceased after 24 hours.

The situation in our *maline* was becoming more and more unbearable. The walls were dripping with our condensed breath. We were in complete darkness, there was not enough air, and we were suffocating. One of us, Gutman, lost his mind. He had a knife and injured at random first my father, then a woman who was lying next to him on the ground. We were all seized by panic. We could not shoot him, it would have made too much noise. He and his wife who had begun screaming were therefore killed with bricks. We buried their two small children's heads under pillows in order to conceal the scene from them and prevent them from crying. Perelka Esterowicz, Michael Good's mother, and her parents were there, in our *maline*. We shall find out about Michael's role in the last chapter.

After 48 hours, the situation outside seemed to have calmed down. We absolutely could not stand it anymore: there was not enough air to breathe and we were so thirsty we were licking the walls. We held a meeting and decided that those who wished to could come out.

A dozen of us chose to emerge, including me and my father. We opened the *maline* that night and walked in an Indian file past the block and towards the wheat fields. We heard shots—probably drunken Lithuanians on guard—and ran and hid in the fields. The shooting ceased. It was impossible to tell whether some of the fugitives were killed or injured.

The next morning, I took off my father's trousers, which had stiffened with blood. He was injured in the buttocks. We remained in that field for another 48 hours with nothing to drink or eat. We heard cannon shots in the distance: the Soviets were probably coming. At the break of dawn, we decided to go to the hospital where my mother was. The streets were deserted: there were no Germans, not a single soul anywhere. The reunion with my mother remains to this day unforgettable. We washed, ate, and my father was attended to. After three long days, on July 13, 1944, the Red Army finally arrived. My father's imprisonment by the Soviets was forgotten: we threw ourselves at the Russian soldiers and kissed them from head to toe. We were finally free! Free, yet homeless, penniless, and with no spare clothes. But we had to wait and see.

***

While we were working at the HKP camp for the Nazi war machine, nearby in Ponary forest, about forty Jewish slaves were scrupulously erasing Nazi crimes before the Russians' arrival. Under the supervision of the SS, bodies were being unearthed and burned. Layers of wood were superimposed with layers of bodies, then sprayed with gasoline and lit up. During the months of hard labor, Jews were digging a tunnel every night with whatever scant means they could find (spoons essentially). A few managed to escape at the last minute; others were caught and killed. Three of the survivors, including the brothers Zaidel and Dagin, went to Israel after the liberation. Their story shocked not only the members of the Association of Vilna Jews in Tel-Aviv, but also the entire country.

***

In 2000, I joined a group of Israelis and Americans on their visit to Vilnius. There were not enough rooms in the hotel, so I had to share my room with another man. We were chatting when I asked him about his name. "My name is Shmuel Gutman, I come from Israel," he replied. "My father and my mother were killed in the *maline* at the HKP camp." It was the son of the man who had lost his mind and had injured my father! He knew his parents had died there, but did not know why or how since we had hidden his and his sister's face beneath pillows.

The man seemed quite emotional already, but when I told him how it all happened, he understandably burst out into tears. He explained to me that he and his sister survived, but that she died of an illness in Czechoslovakia in 1946. Shmuel Gutman never left me for one second during the eight days we were in Vilnius.

This is how a dictatorship produces murderers, sometimes even amongst the educated and the cultivated. Today, seventy years after the tragedy, we can only lament the fact that such regimes still exist all around the world. Alas, we rarely learn from history or the experience of others.

Chapter Five
Liberation, Vilnius, and Lodz
(1944~1949)

Our survival and liberation were an unimaginable miracle for us. Under normal circumstances, such an event is usually lavishly celebrated with champagne. Alas, we were far from having such fantasies. We owned nothing: we did not have a home, money, or any spare clothes. We ate with the Soviet soldiers, but they did not have much either. Besides, the war was still raging. The Soviets' hatred towards the German invader was tremendous. Only 200 to 300 out of the 65,000 Vilnius Jews survived: those who had hidden (like us), the partisans, and the rare survivors from German concentration camps.

We went back to the camp on Subocz Street hoping to recover some personal belongings. Almost everything, however, had disappeared: the plunderers had already been there. My parents rented a room from a Polish lady who lived alone on Tatarska Street. We promised her that she would be paid as soon as we managed to contact our family. We had not heard from them for years. We did not know where our relatives were or who had survived on my mother's side. They had scattered all over the world. We knew that there were no survivors on my father's side, with the exception of the Riwkes cousins, who had been deported to Siberia.

We were liberated on July 13, 1944, but the war continued after that. We were not expecting a second miracle when it happened. My cousin Senia Badasz from Moscow arrived in Vilnius with the Soviet army. Thanks to his father Yuli's connections, Senia, an only child, had been able to avoid the battlefield. He was happy to find us alive. Russians knew what the Nazis had done to Jews in occupied territories. He told us that the Wojczyks, my aunt's family, were alive and well and that Maurice was studying in Moscow. He also told us that the Riwkes were faring well in Siberia. Looking back, we can only cherish their luck to have been deported to Siberia: had they stayed in Vilnius, they would never have survived.

Senia informed us that Grisza and his wife Riwa had left Belgium when the Germans arrived and that they were currently in Mexico, where Riwa had relatives. As for Boris, he and his family had taken refuge in Switzerland. He also told us about his confrontation with the NKVD. In order to contact Grisza in Mexico, Senia turned to the Mexican embassy in Moscow. The ambassador's Russian girlfriend, however, worked for the NKVD and denounced him. He was accused of committing "treason against the fatherland" and was sent to the salt mines where he met Solzhenitsyn. When the war began, he was released along with many other prisoners and promoted officer.

Senia helped us financially and thanks to him we found a glimmer of hope. My parents and I were very lucky to speak Russian as he spoke only that language, in contrast to his parents who spoke perfect Yiddish (his mother was from Riga, Latvia). Senia was aware of our intention to go to the West. He would have liked to come as well, but his parents' destiny forbade him even to think about it. They would have surely been sent to Siberia.

Our goal was to retrieve our belongings from the Pole who had taken them and had never contacted us again. Having a relative in the Soviet army was an important advantage. We went looking for the Pole with Senia and another Russian soldier. We found him at home and got back our belongings. We took our revenge by turning his apartment upside down.

We remained in Vilnius for about six months. Meanwhile, my fathers' cousins the Riwkes returned from Siberia. They found the gold buried in their basement, yet not the diamonds. The Riwkes spent months looking for the wooden cupboard and yet could not find it. They hid the gold once again in a wooden trunk that my father made, in view of a future departure. With the exception of a communist minority, Jewish survivors and Soviet ex-prisoners generally intended to leave Lithuania. Everyone wanted to go West, but timing was key as the Soviets were about to close the borders after the war. Lodz was often chosen as an intermediary stage since it was the best-preserved Polish city and it was therefore easier to find housing there.

While we were considering how and when to go to Lodz, the Wojczyks (my mother's sister and her family) arrived from the Soviet Union and decided to come with us. We thus arrived in Lodz in early 1945 and everyone rented a flat. We found lodging at 57 Legionow Street, on the first floor. On the ground floor there was another family of Wilno survivors, the Sakins. They eventually emigrated to France, like us. Every family then decided upon a destination: the Riwkes chose to go to Israel and the Wojczyks to Belgium, where Mania and her husband, Samuel, had a brother each and where their son Maurice could finish the studies he had begun in Moscow.

Meanwhile, the war ended on May 8, 1945. We were immensely happy. I shall never forget Yuri Levitan's announcement of the end of the war on behalf of Stalin, broadcast on the Soviet radio. I was deeply moved by his speech, which I still have on my computer today.

As soon as the war ended, concentration camp survivors and ex-prisoners returned home to look for possible survivors. Most of them were disappointed, but some found their relatives and planned their departure. Such was the case of my friend Meier Shapiro, who found his mother and sister in Vilnius, but not his father. From 1946 onward, most concentration camp survivors lived in Displaced Persons (DP) camps set up by the Allied Anglo-American forces in Germany before selecting their final destination.

My parents and I had decided to stay in Lodz for the moment and to see what happened. I enrolled in high school and resumed my studies after years of interruption. I was a head taller and several years older than my classmates. I skipped two grades every year. The high school was attended mostly by Poles and a few rare Jews. One day a Polish student shouted at a Jewish girl: "I don't like Jews, I prefer Germans!" I broke a chair over his back, was dismissed from school, and accepted again a couple of weeks later. I got my high school diploma, *matura,* in 1947, when I was twenty years old. I then began studying engineering at Lodz University of Technology.

My parents earned their living by trading in food and clothing items. My mother was the one who took the lead. The *yiddishe mame*, who appeared to be entirely devoted to her husband and only son *Shleimele*, became a businesswoman. She traded in food in Germany and came back with clothes that she sold in Poland. Still, we did not intend at all to stay in Poland. My friend Meier Shapiro wrote to me that there were more than forty Jewish students in Munich, assisted by the American Jewish Joint Distribution Committee, and that the atmosphere was good. He specified that German diplomas were recognized in the United States. My parents consented to my decision to go finish my studies in Munich.

Later, in 1950, my parents received a visa from Grisza in Mexico, which allowed them to emigrate to France.

Chapter Six
University Years in Munich
(1949–1952)

I spent four semesters at Lodz University of Technology and then decided to finish my studies in Munich, which was nonetheless just a stage for me: I wanted to flee Europe and go further west, to the United States.

People have often asked me why I chose Germany to complete my studies. The answer is simple. My family did not want to remain in Poland, my German was good enough, and besides, Jewish students were given financial support by the Joint Committee. Enrolling in German universities was also easier due to the war.

The choice of countries was limited. There was France and the United Kingdom, of course, but they were both unfamiliar to us and we did not speak the languages. Eastern Europe had been under German influence for centuries: it was common for Eastern Europeans to go there to study or to have medical treatment. My maternal grandmother, for instance, had cancer treatment in Berlin long before the war.

The university in Munich accepted me as a transfer student without any difficulty. The university administration was open and helpful due to the war (a war that caused more than 50 million deaths). I enrolled at *Technische Hochschule München* (TH) as a third-year student in electronics. In the beginning, I stayed with our friends from Wilno, the Singers. They had two daughters. Assia and her husband Bomka Genichowicz were both studying stomatology at the university. The younger one, Ida, was single. Their parents lived at the DP camp in Feldafing, 20 kilometers south of Munich. The two daughters lived in Munich to be closer to the university and I shared a flat with them. Even though I was considered part of the family, I still had to sleep in the cold kitchen.

We were not obliged to stay in the DP camp, so everyone who could afford it lived in Munich, Germany's best-preserved city. There were DP camps everywhere in Germany and more than 250,000 Jewish and other prisoners liberated from concentration camps who had to be accommodated. Created in 1946 by the the Allied forces, DP camps sometimes lasted until 1956. Some concentration camp prisoners returned home to look for survivors and then came back to Germany disappointed before leaving for their final destination. The majority of Jews emigrated to the United States and Israel; a minority came to France. There were a few DP camps in Italy as well. That is where Michael Good's parents ended up going (I shall talk about that later). Wowka Gdud and Perelka Esterowicz, both originally from Wilno, studied medicine in Rome. After graduation, they emigrated to the United States and married there.

ORT played an important role in DP camps by providing young people and adults with the professional training that allowed them to find work and earn a living once they arrived at their final destination. The proverb "give a man a fish and you feed him for a day; teach a man to fish and you feed him for a lifetime" nicely illustrates the organization's purpose. As briefly mentioned in Chapter One, the ORT educational institution was founded in Saint Petersburg in 1880 by rich Jewish benefactors, such as Baron Horace de Günzburg. Its initial purpose was to give poor Jews under

Tsarist Russia the opportunity to learn a trade. The acronym ORT in Russian, stands for "Association for the Promotion of Skilled Trades." It had a dazzling success in Russia and quickly spread in the west. As a result of the political events in Europe and the Soviet Union, ORT headquarters moved from Saint Petersburg to Berlin, then Paris up until Hitler's arrival, and finally London, where they are still today.

While I was studying in Munich, my parents left Lodz and moved to Paris in 1950. The Wojczyks were already in Brussels, where Maurice had completed his degree, while the Riwkes had opened a jewelry store in Tel Aviv. Representatives of Israeli Zionist organizations had come to Germany and were encouraging Jews to emigrate to Israel. Where did Germany stand in terms of the Jewish question? Did Germans feel ashamed? Neither Germans nor Jews talked about the past. Everyone was struggling to rebuild their life and was thinking about the future.

I felt comfortable in Germany and this is all that mattered to me. All I wanted was to live and complete my education. Occasionally I had to pair with a German friend but we never talked about politics. German students were roughly my age because they had lost a few years doing their military service before they could go to university. Jewish shops in Munich reopened, mostly on Möhlstrasse. I did not feel any anti-Semitism. Everyone was healing their wounds. Germany suffered great human losses too.

My friends Singer and Genichowicz, who hosted me upon my arrival in Munich, finished their studies. They were both dentists. Both families left Munich in 1951 and went to the United States. I found myself alone and rented a room from a German lady not far from Max-Joseph-Platz. With my friend Bomka, who was older and smarter than me, we ran a business and earned a bit of money. This allowed me to rent a room and make ends meet. My uncle Boris from Belgium also helped me a little, but my major source of income was the American Joint.

Jewish students in Munich in 1951.
Arnold (far right) and I (far left) are sitting on the ground.

One early morning, I looked through my window and saw a troop of Wehrmacht soldiers in the street. I was terrified and immediately called my landlady. She reassured me that they were shooting a film. I quickly came to myself, but the event remained engraved in my memory.

During my stay in Munich, there were between forty and fifty Jewish students who came from different Eastern European countries (mainly from Poland). Many of them lacked parents or even family. They were studying medicine and stomatology at the university or structural and electrical engineering at the TH. I chose electronics because I could see a future in it. And I was right because over the last fifty years there has been tremendous progress in this field. I had outstanding professors, all of them researchers, who worked in the industry and taught at the same time. One of them was Professor Mainke, who worked at Telefunken and taught at TH.

We spoke mostly Polish since not all Jewish students from Poland spoke Yiddish. We spoke German with other Jewish students. We also addressed each other by first name. Mine was Schlamek (Szloma in Polish). Three of my best friends—Marek, Arontchik, and Kuba—eventually emigrated to the United States. Marek became Mark Hupert and entered construction. Arontchik Kerszkowski became professor Arnold Kerr, a railway specialist. Kuba or Jacob Stern was a physician. He died in 2006 and left behind a wife and two children.

Most students lived in the city where they either rented a room or shared a flat. We used to see each other every day at the university cafeteria. Outside of the classroom, I would sometimes study with Juzek Lieberman. Whenever we could, we met on Sundays; the rest of the time we studied at home. Thanks to the American Joint Committee's material help and food and cigarette parcel supplies, we had a fairly good life, which was usually better than that of German students. On Sunday nights, we usually went to the lively Schwabing neighborhood. Jewish students organized a ball once or twice every year; we all shared the profits.

Since I arrived in Germany in the middle of my studies, I had to repeat my fifth semester and thus stay in Munich six more months. After my final exams, I wrote my *Diplomarbeit* (thesis), which allowed me to obtain my engineering degree in 1952. My parents had meanwhile settled in Paris and were tired of emigrating and living out of suitcases. They insisted that I, their only son, go join them in Paris. I was about to experience a series of new challenges: learn a new language, discover a new country, and search for work. But how could I have left my parents alone? It was unthinkable: I was their only son, the apple of my mother's eye.

I remained in touch with my friends who went to the United States. We met several times during my business trips to Portland, Oregon. The last time we met was in New York in May 2012, before a World ORT meeting in Washington DC I had to attend.

Alas, my friends grow fewer and fewer. Arnold died soon after his wife Berta Kerr had told me he was bedridden and that his days were numbered. I attended his funeral in Delaware on May 30, 2012. Mark's wife, Cesia, who had a brilliant career as a doctor and became the head of an American clinic, has Alzheimer's and has completely lost her memory now.

What an injustice: we used to tell ourselves that if we survived the war, we were never going to die. Alas, Our Supreme Judge is not listening to us.

Chapter Seven
Paris
(1952-1961)

My parents arrived in Paris in 1950 with a big
wooden suitcase they had brought from Vilnius.
They did not speak a word of French. At first, they
stayed at a hotel, which was paid for by the Joint
Committee and the Casip-Cojasor Foundation.[16]
There were many Polish Jews in Belleville
(small part of Paris) back at the time. My mother
immediately knew what she had to do: she
bought clothes (shmates) and sold them to people
who spoke her languages (Russian, Yiddish, and
Polish).

As for my father, he got into neon lighting,
which back in the 1950s was a new energy-
efficient technology. He bought one neon light,
dismounted it, and quickly understood how it
worked. He could then make the transformer
and the support himself and buy the rest of the
hardware. The technical part was fine, but one
could not start a business without having a work
permit or speaking French. My father looked for
an associate and found Max, a young French Jew

[16] Casip-Cojasor Fondation is a French institution directed
by the Rothschilds. It assists poor and handicapped Jews.

who spoke Yiddish and was interested in the project. The business slowly took off. Max bought the necessary material and sold the ready-to-use neon lights. My father produced the transformer and the metal support, on which he mounted the remaining parts, such as the glass tube and the starter. They used to buy Mazda and Philips glass tubes from a retailer. Abram and Max's business took off and was quite successful.

After two years, Max already knew how to make neon lighting himself and thought he did not need my father anymore, so he sent him away. My father could not do anything about it from a legal point of view as nothing was in his name and he lacked a work permit. Back then, if I remember correctly, one had to have a ten-year residence permit to be eligible for a work permit. Such was the life of an emigrant without any documents, language, or rights. My father was shocked and deeply disappointed. The incident was yet another frustration in his life.

When I arrived in Paris in 1952, my father was still working with Max. My parents had left the hotel and had rented a small apartment near Jourdain metro station. I stayed with them and slept on the wooden Wilno suitcase. My mother could already make herself understood in French, my father less so. I did not speak any French at all. As soon as I arrived in Paris, I enrolled at the Alliance Française. My parents knew quite a few people already. They were more than a little proud of their prodigal son who had returned home with a degree in engineering.

"Jews should help each other," a friend of my parents once said. "Your son is an engineer. I shall introduce him to a very nice man, whose name is Paul Agynski. He will find him work." Soon after, I met the man in question: he was born in Lodz and spoke very good Polish. He had come to France well before the war to pursue his education and graduated from Grenoble Electrical Engineering Institute. He was very lucky to have chosen France. Most students went to study in Germany. Paul Agynski came to France with his brother and, along with one more associate, opened a factory in the Parisian suburb Montreuil called LIE (Laboratoire Industriel d'Electricité).

When I finished my course at the Alliance Française, Paul Agynski introduced me to the Fis brothers, who owned the company Omega in Vincennes (another Parisian suburb). André and Boris Fis were Russian Jews who had been living in France for a long time. Omega produced radio and television set components (there was no color TV yet). They sold the components to manufacturers, who assembled television and radio sets: a bit like my father with the neon lighting, but on a whole different scale.

I began working for Omega in 1953. I was in the television department and dealt with tuners and the MF (Medium Frequency) part of the television set. My boss, Mr. Tarrel, explained to me what I was supposed to do, but spoke so fast I did not understand a thing. I still nodded in agreement, while a colleague was listening behind the door so that he could explain the instructions to me afterwards. I was sweating like a pig. One can hardly imagine how frustrating it is not to understand the language in such a context.

Georges, an elderly Russian, was the head of the workshop. He helped me a lot in the beginning. I had two problems: the language and the lack of experience. I had not heard a word about television or transistors at the TH in Munich, but things got better and I was becoming more and more autonomous with time. There was a pleasant atmosphere at the lab and I was on very good terms with my colleagues. I bought my first car, a Renault 4CV, and could go down the Route Nationale 7 all the way to the Côte d'Azur (the French Riviera) and admire the region's beauty.

The television business soared and the factory's owner, Andre Fis, decided to hire an engineering advisor, Mr. Delaitre, who appreciated my work. My colleagues were all experienced technicians, yet, unlike me, they lacked theoretical background. Soon, Mr. Delaitre offered me a position at Ribet & Desjardins in

Montrouge near Paris. As soon as I was hired in 1956, I quit my job at Omega after nearly three years.

Ribet & Desjardins was also a television set and measuring equipment manufacturer. I began working in the measuring devices department and was supposed to develop a vobulator (a part of a television set's control system). For more than a year, I worked in addition on weekends as engineering advisor for a company that produced transistor radios. The company was in Puteaux and belonged to Paul Agynski's friend Georges Nissen. I worked for Ribet and Desjardins for five years before another opportunity came my way in 1961.

My parents' life also changed drastically. In 1953, the German government headed by Chancellor Konrad Adenauer granted compensations (*Wiedergutmachung*) to people who had been persecuted by the Nazis. We received a monthly sum and a backdated block amount. This allowed my parents to live comfortably. They rented a nice apartment on 6 rue Lamblardie, in the 12th district of Paris, and did not need to work anymore. They could afford to go on vacation and visit members of the family, such as Mania and Boris in Belgium, my mother's older brother Grisza and his wife Riwa, who had left Mexico and had settled in Israel, as well as my father's cousins, the Riwkes.

Israel, 1960.
My parents, my
uncle Grisza, Riwa,
and I standing
behind them.

A few years after Stalin's death, between 1958 and 1960, the Russian side of my mother's family left Moscow. A special agreement allowed Jews to leave the Soviet Union and emigrate to Israel. The entire Badasz family thus arrived in Vienna, but they did not intend to go to Israel. Uncle Yuli and his wife Liza decided to go to Brussels, where they joined Yuli's brother Boris and sister Mania. Their son Senia settled in Bad Ems, Germany with his wife and son. My cousin Maurice Woitchik (Mania's son) joined the STIB (Brussels Intercommunal Transport Company, which built the Brussels metro) and was promoted chief engineer. When he retired, he wrote a memoir, *Du transsibérien au métro de Bruxelles* (*From the Trans-Siberian Railway to the Brussels Metro*). The Trans-Siberian is, of course, a reference to the time when the Wojczyks fled Rovno upon the Germans' arrival and took refuge in the Soviet Union.

With the exception of my university years in Germany, I have always lived with my parents. Oddly, we never spoke about the past, about that dark period in our lives. Today I would have asked them many questions, but unfortunately, they are not alive any more. My mother died in 1987, my father about a year later in 1988.

Chapter Eight
Work, Family, and Homeland
(1961–2012)

My spiritual father, Paul Agynski, had an old Romanian friend, Maurice Parisier, who, like Paul, had come to France to study. He was graduated from the prestigious engineering school Supélec (Ecole supérieure d'électricité). Parisier lived in New York and owned the Parisian firm RTI (Relations techniques intercontinentales), which represented a number of American companies. Businessman on the look-out as he was, he carefully followed the development of American electronics companies. He learned that Tektronix in Portland, Oregon was producing quality measuring equipment, which was selling rather well.

Parisier went to Portland, met with Tektronix's President Howard Volum, and obtained the distribution of his products in France. Francis Mafarette was RTI's sales manager and Parisier's good friend of many years, Miron Kaplan, took care of RTI's finances as a part-time job. Tektronix products were well received on the market and Parisier had to hire new staff for the new product line. Maurice met Paul and it happened that they talked about me.

I met Parisier in June 1961. We got along very well: I was the right man for the job considering my background, age, and experience. He asked me, however, whether I spoke English, as all product manuals were in that language and it was necessary to meet with Tektronix engineers from time to time. I had to admit that I did not speak English, but that I was going to speak it in three months time when I was supposed to start.

I kept my word. I went to London, where I signed up at the English Tuition Center and studied for 10 hours every day. In the evenings, I looked for opportunities to practice English. I came back to Paris reinvigorated. Parisier was surprised to hear me speak English that was at least as good as his was. I quit Ribet & Desjardins after five years. I learned a lot with them and the experience would serve me well at my new job.

In September 1961, I started working for RTI as technical manager. There were already a dozen technicians in the sales and repair departments. I was gradually becoming familiar with the measuring equipment. The Americans who worked at Tektronix, however, were more interested in sales than in service. Francis Mafarette's English was not that good and he was not a technician either, so I began attending meetings more often. At first, my job consisted mainly in supervising repairs, but little by little I began concluding maintenance contracts, which led to meeting with customers. As Tektronix sales were growing fast, it was necessary to hire more sales and after-sales staff. I was thus in charge of recruiting as well as training. My work was quite varied, absorbing, and fascinating.

Charles Schulman, Harry Kramer, and Gérard Haymann were some of my Parisian friends. We often met on Sundays to have a drink on the Champs Elysées and chase girls. We also used to go dancing in Saint-Germain-des-Pres. Bit by bit, I began enjoying my youth, which had been virtually nonexistent during my years of studying and working. I also became a French citizen in 1962 (hence the word "homeland" in the chapter's title). I followed Gérard's advice and Gallicized my name to Simon-François.

I sometimes visited my spiritual father, Paul Agynski, at his office or at his home in Sceaux (about 10 kilometers south of Paris). We had tea and cakes prepared by his German wife, who spoke to me in German. Paul was a Zionist and was very fond of Israel, where part of his family lived. He was in Spain during the war and had many friends there. Paul had friends everywhere. The Agynskis had two daughters, both of them married. I am still in touch with one of them, Marianne, and her husband, Charles Funk. They are both physicians.

I was 35 years old and used to go out at night to make up for my lost youth. My *yiddishe mame*, however, kept reproaching me for my bohemian lifestyle: she wanted me to have a family and gave me as an example my cousin Maurice in Brussels, who was married and had two children already. It then happened that my friend Harry Kramer introduced me to Francine Levy.

The Kramers were watch wholesalers. They worked with a jewelry shop, which Francine had inherited from her deceased parents. Francine was single and her cousin Andrée, a middle-aged unmarried woman, was running the shop. Francine lived with her uncle Roger Lerner and his wife Micheline. She was a pretty brown-eyed brunette of medium height. She was intelligent, stylish, and cultivated, had studied law in Paris and had earned a Bachelor of Arts degree from Worcester State University. Her father had got caught in a roundup in 1942, while her mother had slipped through the cracks, yet had died prematurely after the war. I liked Francine a lot. We had much in common and went out for a short while before we decided to get married in 1963.

We had a nice big wedding with many guests on Francine's side and, alas, only a few on my side besides my parents and several friends and colleagues. My boss Maurice Parisier was there. We had become friends even though he was a cautious man, who did not trust people easily. He gave me a nice wedding gift.

Francine had a small apartment on Rue des Vignes where we settled after we got married. Our daughter Nathalie was born there in 1965. A few years later we moved to a bigger apartment nearby, on Rue du Ranelagh, close to RTI where I worked. How can I describe my feelings for Francine? Our relationship was one of mutual security and trust. It was a tender and, I think, loving relationship. We had many friends, most of them old friends of Francine's, whom we saw regularly, yet also wished to find something we could do together. Brigitte Weil from Besançon, who had in the meantime become Gérard Heymann's wife, thought of golf. After some discussion, we unanimously adopted the idea and all of us signed for golf lessons.

Tektronix products became more sophisticated with time and customers often requested assistance. The training I offered helped sales increase considerably and I became more and more known among customers. One day, Professor Armbruster from the University of Strasbourg suggested that I do a thesis in the brand new field of sampling, which allows one to observe ultra fast electrical signals on an oscilloscope screen. After two years of research, I earned a PhD in Engineering while working at RTI.

The business was evolving rapidly. In 1965, Tektronix decided to establish itself in France without a retailer like RTI. Shrewd businessman as he was, Parisier tried to add value to his business. He hired the Polytechnique graduate and former pilot Charles Billet as Managing Director and made me Sales Manager. I do not know what the transaction amount was, but Parisier had nothing to complain about.

My wedding with Francine.

Tektronix constructed a large building next to Hewlett Packard at Ulis (30 kilometers southwest of Paris) and moved the entire staff that worked on their products from RTI there. Instead of three kilometers, I now had to commute 30 kilometers to go to work every morning, but it did not really matter since I loved the job.

Tektronix kept growing: it set up branches in other French cities to increase its market shares. Two Englishmen were in charge of Tektronix Europe: Don Alvey, based in the United States, and his friend Frank Doyle in Guernsey Island, UK, where Tektronix had a factory. We had to hire sales engineers and maintenance technicians for each new branch in Lyon, Nice, and Toulouse. Simon-François had a lot on his plate.

It was not easy to find competent staff back then, but neither is it today. We recruited engineers via job ads and technicians from AFPA (National Agency for Adults' Professional Training). Teachers there knew me well and introduced me to competent people. After a while, we rented premises in different cities and trained the new staff in Paris. The business soared. I often went to Portland with Francine. The trips were pleasant and Francine spoke perfect English. Once, an American friend of mine took us in his airplane to Las Vegas. I had good contacts at the Portland factory and must say, with no false modesty, that I was appreciated on all levels there.

Since I had never received any sales or marketing training, I went to Brussels to do a training course. Later on I even wrote a book for internal use: *The Sales Engineer in an Integrated Marketing Environment*. The marketing aspect of the job was quite important as sales engineers were supposed to give feedback about customers' reactions to our products as well as our competitors' products—for instance, Hewlett Packard. I had this fascinating and varied job for eight years when a new opportunity came my way.

Tektronix had a factory called Telequipment in London. It produced low-cost devices that never sold as expected. I met with the director of Tektronix Europe and the factory's manager, Bob Groom, in London. I was appointed Head of European Marketing with the mission to boost sales and increase our market share. The goal was achieved after substantial product modification three years later. I worked in London during the week and used to return to Paris on weekends. While I was working in London, I traveled to different countries to visit our retailers, hear reactions to our new products, and give them ideas how to enhance sales.

In 1976, Tektronix decided to phase out gradually our European distributors as it had previously done in France. The countries in question were Italy, Spain, Germany, and Austria. Who was the right man for the job? Naturally, I knew him well: it was Simon or Mister Tektronix, as the Americans used to call me. My new job consisted in selecting personnel of the distributor staff that were apt to join the new Tektronix branches. It was a delicate mission as we had to avoid alienating the distributor and offending its staff.

Our European managers Don and Frank were in charge of financial negotiations with the distributor. While I had to deal with the staff, including sales and after-sale managers, my superiors chose the new General Manager. We then had to rent and equip new premises and assist the branch in its adjustment to Tektronix standards. The process took varying amounts of time, depending on the country. I experienced some difficulties in Italy due to the prevailing culture there which made it difficult to discern true from false. On the other hand, in Spain everything was straightforward: one could trust Spanish people. I had a pleasant time in Madrid, where I often saw flamenco shows in the evenings.

Our financial director in Spain was an Englishman. One day, I was walking down the street with our General Manager Luis Calvo. We met a typical long-haired, dark-eyed brunette. That evening the financial director Derek Weis invited me for dinner. The same brunette whom I had met earlier on the street opened the door. She spoke perfect French and took me by the hand to show me around the apartment. I noticed several magnificent paintings and asked her who had painted them. She surprised me by saying that they were hers. I was dying to learn more. While we were having a drink in the living room, I asked Derek how he had come to Spain and how he had met his wife. I was once again surprised to learn that they had met in a kibbutz in Israel while Derek was on a one-year sabbatical leave. I asked Maria-Grazia if she was Jewish; she told me she was a Marrano. In 1492, when Jews had to either flee Spain or convert to Catholicism, her family chose to convert themselves, yet they did so only in appearance: part of her family had remained Jewish. That is one of those extraordinary stories that can happen only to Jews.

After Italy and Spain, I went to Germany. The company there was much larger, with many branches and a huge staff, which made my task more complicated. The internationally known firm Rohde & Schwarz was in charge of distribution. I was on excellent terms with the management and stayed in Germany for three years to help the branch take off. My work in Austria was different, since we re-exported Tektronix products from Vienna to Eastern Europe.

I dedicated about ten years of my life to these four countries, going back and forth between them and Paris.

Tektronix kept expanding, which lasted for another dozen of years before it began declining due to its managers' lack of vision in terms of technological innovation. Any electronics company that did not make a proper transition to IT was doomed sooner or later. Tektronix's management considered it inappropriate to compete with their biggest clients who were in the computer field. This point of view signed the company's death warrant. Hewlett Packard's decision, on the other hand, propelled our main competitor to success.

Tektronix had another factory in the Netherlands and decided to open a European marketing center in Amsterdam. The goal was to help the newly created branches become more efficient and increase sales. So they turned to me again. I was 56 years old and available to take up the responsibility. I had known the director of international marketing, the American John Landis, for a long time. I agreed to do the job under the condition that I could retire after four years. The company rented an apartment for me in Amsterdam and bought me a BMW 525.

We hired product managers who were then trained at the main factory in Portland. When visiting branches, we worked with each sales director and tried to find ways of improving sales and market share. The job was fascinating and we managed to obtain results thanks to this cooperation. I received stock options that were exercisable after five years. However, as I mentioned earlier, the company was slowly shrinking and the stock options' value did not increase, not even by one cent.

I used to go back to Paris fairly often. My daughter, Nathalie, was growing up and saw her father only rarely. For many years, Francine played the roles of both mother and father. While I was in Amsterdam in 1987, my dear mother passed away after a long month suffering at the Rothschild Hospital in Paris. I went to see her many times, but the poor woman could not say a word since she had tubes in her mouth. She was buried in the Vilna section of Bagneux cemetery.

Towards the end of 1987, I was 60 years old and, in keeping with our agreement, had to leave Amsterdam and return to Paris. The new General Manager was an ex-sales engineer I had hired previously. He had asked me to help him build new premises. I agreed to do it, but only as a part-time engagement, so that I could at last retire after one year. Eventually, I stayed for almost two years.

Events never come one at a time, so my professional activity and my marriage both ended at the same time. At the end of my stay in Amsterdam, I bought a small apartment and moved in as soon as I came back from the Netherlands. The day after having had dinner with my father one evening in 1988, I received a call from the building manager where my father lived. He informed me that my father was not opening the door. When I arrived, I found him dead in his bed. He joined my mother in the same grave.

I found myself in the big and beautiful city of Paris with no wife, job, or parents. Fortunately, despite our separation, Francine and I remained on good terms. She could always rely on me as

Denise and I.

a friend. My parents had been lucky to have seen me married and could rejoice in the birth of our daughter, Nathalie.

In 1990, I met Denise Malet. She had been divorced for ten years and had two grown-up children, one of them already married. Soon after we met, she came to live with me in my small apartment. As Denise's office was in the city center and my apartment on the outskirts of Paris, I decided to buy a bigger flat at 26 Rue Dagorno in the 12th district of Paris, close to Rue Lamblardie, where my parents used to live.

Denise was very actively involved in various Jewish organizations, which pleased me since my parents contributed to KKL (Jewish National Fund) all their lives. Moreover, I have always been attached to Israel, not only because of my past, but also ever since I was involved with the Zionist organization Betar as a child. Denise gave me a lot of attention and warmth too. We got along well on many points and, besides, both of us needed a partner.

My daughter, Nathalie, followed in her mother's footsteps and graduated in law with remarkable results. In 1993, she married

From left to right: Jean-Michel, Denise, Nathalie, and I.

Jean-Michel Koster, an engineer who had entered finance. They had a son, Jeremy, in 1995, and a daughter, Clara, in 1998.

In 1989, I was retired and my spiritual father Paul Agynski was once again there for me as he had always been. Paul was a member of ORT France's Board of Directors for many years. He talked to Jules Bloch, ORT France's General Director at the time, and, with his consent, I joined the association as technical advisor and board member. I was pleasantly surprised by the quality of the board members' volunteer work: President Gilbert Dreyfus (former CEO of Paris Airports), Boris Schneerson (one of Schlumberger's managers), Eliane Roubach, Jean-Hugues Leopold-Metzger from Strasbourg, and William Amselem, among others. They all became friends of mine.

ORT's headquarters are located in Paris, but there are a total of six ORT schools in France with an enrollment of more than 3,000 students. The education these schools offer can be either general or specialized, depending on each school.

After a while, Jules Bloch left ORT. The association's financial situation was critical; it had a deficit of about 6 million dollars. President Gilbert Dreyfus asked Treasurer William Amselem and me to deal with redundancies. After a whole year of difficult negotiations with the schools' directors, seventy people (mostly administrative staff) were dismissed.

Paul Agynski with his wife Alice.

Today I am still a member of ORT, yet my great unforgettable friends Paul Agynski, Eliane Roubach, William Amselem, and Boris Schneerson are all dead. The association is doing well under Lucien Kalfon's presidency and Marc Timsit's management.

The world is changing; we have now fully entered the IT age. Technology is developing faster and faster. At university, I was taught about vacuum tubes. When I began my career, tubes were already outdated and were replaced by transistors. Nowadays they too have become obsolete and have been replaced by chips. I am now trying to understand how computer works, but it seems to me to be more complex than a Boeing 707. Fortunately, the twenty years

I have been retired allowed me to partially resolve the computer mystery.

The internet thus helped me get in touch with survivors all around the globe. After sixty years, I managed to find a few people, who by a miracle had come out of concentration camps alive. Life is an endless circle. I was contacted by the American physician Michael Good, son of Wilno survivors, whose father Wowka Gdud escaped alive from Ponary and mother Perela Esterowicz survived by hiding in the same *maline* as me at the HKP on Subocz Street. In the United States, the Gduds changed their name to Good. They traveled to Vilnius in 1999 to show younger members of the family where they were born, had lived, and suffered: the ghetto, the HKP, and of course Ponary forest, where practically the entire Wilno Jewry lies.

Perela told her son Michael about the events at the HKP and the role that Major Karl Plagge played in the protecting of 500 Jewish workers and their families. More than a 100 of them survived. When he got back to the United States, Michael began researching Holocaust survivors, but above all Karl Plagge in order to thank him on behalf of the survivors. Karl Plagge was in command of the HKP for three years, 1941-1944. He tried to isolate us from the surrounding horror and did all he could to protect us from the SS murderers. Plagge's actions to help us gave us abundant proof of his humanity. The greatest risk he undertook was to take my mother to the city hospital personally. This deed allowed me to obtain the Righteous Medal for him from Yad Vashem in Jerusalem in 2005. The last chapter of this book is entirely dedicated to him.

In his attempt to reconstitute Plagge's life, Michael managed to contact via the internet a few Germans who allowed us to discover facts about Plagge's life and get to know this remarkable man and his life. Unfortunately, Karl Plagge was no longer alive at that time; he died in 1957. New missions await me in Germany: I wonder whether I will one day find the time to retire.

Chapter Nine
Major Karl Plagge
(1897-1957)

During the dark years of the Nazi occupation (1941-1944), my parents and I were inmates in the Vilnius Ghetto. We were slave laborers at the HKP (*Heereskraftfahrpark, Ost 562*) workshops for repairing Wehrmacht military vehicles. From the beginning, Major Karl Plagge was the commander of all workshops around the city. 250 German officers and soldiers, Poles, Russian prisoners, and 500 Jewish forced laborers worked there. This information was not given to us at that time. We rather discovered it over the years, but mostly after the war.

When the Germans arrived in the city and the Gestapo and the SS began performing *Aktions* (mass executions), we understood that Jews were considered to be less than slaves. We were *Untermenschen* or subhumans, who were being beaten for no reason, stamped upon, and murdered everywhere: on the street, in the ghetto, even at work. But we also realized that at the HKP, Jews were decently treated. We did not know why. We had an *Ausweis* (identification card) of the right color, which apparently protected us from the shootings in Ponary.

Our imprisonment can be divided in two periods. While in the ghetto, we did not quite understand that one person could have allowed for a decent attitude not only towards Jews, but towards Polish and Russian prisoners as well. Work at the HKP was overseen by Wehrmacht soldiers, who were far from being as gentle as lambs elsewhere. Our "masters" were the SS and the Wehrmacht paid them per slave's head. Rumor had it in the ghetto that at one point Plagge had gone to the Lukiszki prison with a group of soldiers to reclaim some HKP Jews who had been captured during an *Aktion*. I cannot tell if that were true, as I did not see it myself. If it is true, however, it means that Plagge put himself in danger in front of the SS, which is an heroic deed.

The second period began in September 1943. About two weeks before the ghetto was liquidated, we were transferred to the HKP blocks at 37 Subocz Street. We then had the opportunity to observe Plagge's humanity. He was freer than before as he was more at home in his workshops, despite the fact that officially we were administered by the SS.

Plagge's achievements include:
- Not a single Jew was beaten or maltreated;
- Food was decent, considering the circumstances;
- Plagge made frequent appearances among us, at Subocz Street;
- Following the *Kinder Aktion* (the murder of 200 children on March 27, 1944), Plagge set up a sewing workshop for female inmates in order to preserve them from the SS;
- He managed to send to the eastern front an officer who had told him that, according to the Nazi doctrine, Jews had to be maltreated;
- Plagge took a substantial risk by taking my mother to the city hospital.

These are all positive signs, yet do we know who that man really was? Seen from the outside, Plagge gave the impression of a stiff, unsmiling, and introverted individual. Some said he suspected there might be a traitor working for the Gestapo among us.

Many years after the war, in 2000, I was in Israel to attend an ORT meeting where I met Rabbi Farber. He told me that, while at the HKP blocks, he had once asked Plagge for the permission to make *matzot* (unleavened bread) for Passover and that Plagge had granted it to him. I never thought this story was true, as many legends were circulating about Plagge. Regardless of whether it were true or not, it reveals people's attitude towards him. Even if those stories were all figments of the imagination, they were still based on impressions and feelings that were disclosed later on.

During that same trip to Israel, I saw my friend Marek Swirsky, another Wilno survivor and teacher at ORT Israel. He told me what happened to his father. David Swirsky and Plagge knew each other from the *Technische Hochschule* (Technical Unviersity) in Darmstadt where they both studied. Since he knew Plagge, David was privileged to work at the HKP military kitchen. One day, while we were still living in the ghetto, an SS guard searched Jews as they were leaving the kitchen and found that David had hidden food on himself.

No one knows what could have happened if Plagge were not there. He told the SS: "I'll take care of it." Plagge and his faithful driver took David to a room nearby where they made noises and feigned cries. The driver slightly hit David in the nose to make him bleed a little and then spread the blood over his face. Then they took him back and assured the SS that the Jew had had a good lesson and that he would never do it again. If it were not his son who told me about this adventure, I would never have believed it.

Many years had to pass before one could really learn about this man, his life, and his past. His story was revealed little by little following the Goods' family trip to Vilnius in 1999. Upon his return to the United States, Michael Good, a doctor from New York State whose parents were Wilno survivors, decided to gather as much information about this mysterious man as possible, and, above all, to find and thank him for his deeds. One might think that, in today's digital world, such research would be easy. That is wrong, however, for the quest took more than four years (2000-2004) and became the subject of Michael Good's book, *The Search for Major Plagge: The Nazi Who saved Jews* (*Die Suche: Karl Plagge, der Wehrmachtsoffizier, der Juden rettete*, German translation by Joerg Fiebelkorn). A brief summary of the book follows.

At this point, I would like to express our gratitude to the small group of people in Germany who helped us conduct our research on Plagge. Via the internet, they found out that more than a hundred Jews had survived in Wilno thanks to Karl Plagge. Initially, the group was composed of three members:

- Salomon Klaczko, a Jewish scientist from Montevideo, whose parents were from Wilno. He lived in Hamburg and was Joerg Fiebelkorn's partner;
- Joerg Fiebelkorn, who was a retired officer of the Bundeswehr and in charge of a company for marine GPS devices;
- Dr. Marianne Viefhaus, an archivist at Darmstadt Technical University.

As a former officer, Joerg wrote to the archive collection in Wiesbaden and requested information on Plagge. Soon he learned that Plagge was born in Darmstadt, had fought during World War I, and had been imprisoned. He had also contracted polio and had a stiff leg as a result of it. Plagge was mobilized again during World War II and, being an engineer, was appointed commanding officer of the HKP in Vilnius.

Marianne picked up from there and pursued research in Darmstadt. She found out that Plagge was born in 1897 and had attended high school in Darmstadt. Following his releasing from prison after World War I, he studied mechanical engineering at the Darmstadt Technical University. He had married Anke Madsen, had no children, and had died of a heart attack in 1957.

From left to right: Michael Good, Salomon Klaczko, Marianne Viefhaus, and Joerg Fiebelkorn in 2002.

Marianne then contacted the Chamber of Commerce. The economic situation in Germany in the 1930s was particularly harsh. The unemployed Plagge joined NSDAP (*National Sozialistische Deutsche Arbeiter Partei*, the Nazi Party) in 1931. Since he was highly educated, he was put in charge of training party members. Later, he found work with Hessen Werke in Darmstadt, an electromechanical firm which does not exist today. Marianne met with a member of the Hesse family who remembered Plagge perfectly. In 1937-38, the Nazis had insisted upon the separation of the firm's owner, Kurt Hesse, from his wife, who was half-Jewish. He had refused to do it and was abandoned by all of his friends, with the exception of Plagge and one other man.

Kurt Hesse stepped down from his company's management and passed it over to Plagge. Plagge remained a party member, yet disagreed with NSDAP's racial policies and distanced himself from its ideology. In 1938, Frau Hesse gave birth to a son, Konrad Hesse, whom I met in Jerusalem in 2005 when Plagge was recognized as Righteous Among the Nations. He confirmed Plagge's views on racism and antisemitic laws and told me that Plagge had been shocked by the havoc of Kristallnacht. Konrad Karl Hesse is Plagge's godson.

Lazar Greisdorf, a survivor who lives in Canada, was a ten-year-old boy who had escaped the *Kinder Aktion* at the HKP camp in 1944. In 1948, the Greisdorf family lived in a DP (Displaced Persons) camp in Ludwigsburg near Stuttgart. The Greisdorfs had by chance read in the press about Karl Plagge's denazification trial. They asked a German lady, Frau Eichamüller, to represent them during the proceedings. They told her that they were among many to have survived thanks to Plagge.

Frau Eichamüller testified in his favour. After the trial, Plagge visited the Greisdorfs at the DP camp and spent two nights there. Plagge's joy was beyond words: he had not known there were any HKP survivors. He was happy to learn that over a hundred Jews had survived: it was the best gift he had ever received. Plagge was in a dreadful situation after the war, so the Greisdorfs gave him a parcel of food. What an unexpected turn of events that Jews should be happy to help a German officer. Plagge's thank-you letter to the Greisdorfs (see Appendix) is an exceptional written expression of his joy and humanist values.

During the first years after the war, the Allied forces made members of NSDAP fill in a questionnaire about their role during the conflict as part of denazification trials in occupied Germany. Thanks to the Greisdorfs' intervention, Karl Plagge's record could have been cleansed. Yet, Plagge insisted upon being classified in the fourth lowest category, *Mitläufer* (Follower). There were a total of five categories and "Follower" came fourth between "Less incriminated" and "Exonerated."

Since Marianne Viefhaus's health was deteriorating, two new German members joined our Plagge Gruppe: Hanni (Hannelore) Skroblies, who worked with Marianne at the university, and

Hanni's friend, Christoph Jetter. Hanni found Plagge's wife's cousin, Dr. Madsen from Schleiden, who had preserved Plagge's copious correspondence with a variety of people. A few years later, I received an email from Dr Madsen and we stayed in touch even though we never met, as he could not travel without his son's help.

In one of Plagge's letters to his wife Anke, he covertly describes his discouragement and shame over the atrocities his compatriots were committing in the east (see Appendix). In another group of letters to Strauss, a Jewish lawyer Plagge had met on the train, he describes how horrified and ashamed he was of what he saw in Vilnius during his stay there (1941-1944).

Although Plagge's letters clearly demonstrate that he wrote with ease, he never considered writing a memoir for his compatriots. When Strauss suggests that he write one, Plagge replies that he does not have the time to write. He says he is too busy and digresses into a philosophical aside about the French writer Albert Camus and his novel (La Peste) *The Plague,* which had greatly impressed him when he had read its German translation after the war. It is remarkable that Plagge should feel that way, since he apparently felt comfortable discussing the horrors of the war with Jews and close friends. There is abundant literature on the subject of Nazi crimes, which is mostly written by foreigners or survivors. It would be interesting to know how many Germans have written about atrocities committed during the war.

Plagge's greatest regret was no doubt having voted for the Führer and joined the Nazi party. More than twenty years after the war, this was surely how most Germans felt about their vote, which had led to Germany's destruction, the massacre of many populations, and their cultures' annihilation, as well as to the death of more than 50 million people. All because of a simple vote of confidence for Hitler and his promises, cast without foreseeing his real intentions in time. Regretfully, similar phenomena occur in many countries today.

Dr Madsen had one more letter from Plagge, to SS Colonel Humbert Achamer-Pifrader, commander of the Einsatzgruppe A in Riga, Latvia. They knew each other from Darmstadt, where Pifrader was in charge of the Gestapo. Plagge wrote to Pifrader about the need to preserve the Jewish specialists indispensable to the HKP's functioning. Pifrader eventually gave him the permission to keep his Jewish workers along with their families.

Our German friends and Michael Good wrote a number of emails to Yad Vashem over a period of two years, citing facts about Plagge's behavior and asking to recognize him posthumously as Righteous Among the Nations. They met two refusals for the following reason: "We understand that Plagge was a benevolent man, yet at no point did he risk his own life. He relied on the fact that the German war machine needed Jewish manpower." Among the criteria required by Yad Vashem for the awarding of the honorary title is a proof that the person in question "risked his life to save Jews."

I therefore decided to fly to Jerusalem and meet with Dr. Paldiel, then Director of the Department of the Righteous. I first contacted my friend Jacqueline Rebibo in Jerusalem. She introduced me to Lucien Lazar, a member of the commission, who in turn introduced me to Daniel Fraenkel, an historian at Yad Vashem. I told them all about Plagge's deeds, but above all I insisted upon the fact that he had taken my mother out of the concentration camp and driven her to the city hospital, an action that undeniably put his life at risk. Lazar and Fraenkel promised to back up my request.

On July 23, 2004, Lucien Lazar called me in Paris to tell me that the commission had met the previous day and that, thanks to the brilliant presentation of Fraenkel and another member of the group, Guillade, it had unanimously agreed to posthumously bestow the honorary Righteous Among Nations title on Karl Plagge.

The next issue was who should receive the award, since Plagge did not have any descendants. I suggested Plagge's godson, Konrad Hesse, or an elderly cousin. After much discussion, Avner Shalev,

Chairman of Yad Vashem, suggested Dr. Johann-Dietrich Woerner, president of Darmstadt Technical University. The idea was accepted unanimously.

The ceremony took place in April 2005 in the presence of our German friends and survivors who had come from all corners of the world, with many journalists. Avner Shalev gave the first speech, followed by Woerner and three survivors: Michael Schemiavitz from Israel, Bill Begell from the United States, and me. The ceremony ended with a cocktail in Yad Vashem's garden.

A couple of days later, some of us flew from Jerusalem to Darmstadt, where another ceremony took place in front of an audience of about 400 people, including many key figures. Speeches were given by President Woerner, Darmstadt mayor Peter Benz, and Professor Wette from the University of Freiburg, a specialist in German resistance to Hitler. Two of my friends spoke in English; I was the only one among the survivors to address the audience in German (see Appendix). A few survivors were later interviewed by some German newspapers, resulting in many articles. The Evangelical Sisterhood of Mary in Darmstadt have been sending me their best wishes for the Jewish New Year ever since.

Among the 400 present in Darmstadt, there was the former HKP German soldier Alfons von Deschwanden, accompanied by his daughter Irmgard, a member of our group. The night before the HKP camp was liquidated, Alfons was keeping watch to make sure no one escaped. He saw youths, our friend Bill Begell among them, getting ready to flee, yet did not shoot. During the *Kinder Aktion*, he had hidden a child in the HKP's spare parts warehouse, where many Jews worked and which was under his command. After the war, Alfons was contacted by the child's father, Samuel Taboryski, who had moved to Israel. I visited Alfons in 2006 in Offenburg near the French border. We talked about the HKP in Vilna. We met again in Strasbourg shortly after and spent the day together with our wives, sightseeing and taking pictures. While we were having lunch,

Certificate of Heroes who risked their lives to save Jews from extermination.

I stressed the fact that both of us had been lucky to have worked at the HKP camp: he escaped the eastern front and I escaped Ponary.

All of the above events brought great joy and satisfaction to our *Plagge Gruppe*; our efforts were finally rewarded.

In 2006 my friend and senior officer of the Bundeswehr, Manfred Foehr, succeeded in renaming the military base near Darmstadt as Major-Karl-Plagge-Kaserne. More than 150 guests, mostly military officers, attended the inauguration ceremony. General Treche, my friend Joerg Fiebelkorn, and I gave speeches.

In 2008, Karl Plagge was awarded the gold medal by the Carnegie Foundation for his humane behaviour and saving many human lives.

Around that time, one of Plagge's cousins, Dr. Marianne Wrobel, appeared unexpectedly and joined our group. In 2009, Marianne

Marianne Wrobel and Denise are standing in front of the memorial stele in Ponary which commemorates HKP Jews murdered upon the camp's liquidation in 1944 (2009).

joined me along with 40 Israelis on a trip to Vilnius for the March of the Living.

We visited the HKP blocs on Subocz Street and Marianne laid flowers at the monument commemorating the victims, discovered in their hiding places and shot on the spot. The following day a ceremony took place in Ponary where 100,000 people had been killed and where Marianne laid flowers once again. I stood next to her at all times in order to support her given the stress.

Marianne and her family also joined us on a second trip to Israel in 2010. Our small *Plagge Gruppe* was received by the Association of Vilna Jews in Tel-Aviv at *Beit Vilna* (Vilna House) where a ceremony took place in the presence of the Lithuanian Ambassador to Israel, Darius Degutis. The following day, we visited Yad Vashem, where there was another ceremony in the presence of the German Ambassador to Israel.

In the above picture, taken in 2009, Marianne Wrobel and Denise are standing in front of the memorial stele in Ponary. The President of Lithuania and the Israeli Ambassador were also present at the March of the Living that year.

The stele was replaced after the restoration of Lithuania's independence in 1990. Previously, the stele's Russian inscription read that 100,000 Soviet citizens had been executed by the Nazis, yet did not mention Jewish victims. Marianne also laid flowers at another, smaller stele in Ponary, which commemorates HKP Jews murdered upon the camp's liquidation in 1944.

Marianne has remained active and works to keep the memory of the Vilnius massacres alive among young Lithuanians. I deeply admire her courage and devotion.

Meanwhile, the energetic Hanni and Christoph made four big panels, on which they glued pictures of survivors and Plagge along with descriptions. The meeting in Darmstadt and the press coverage had such a broad impact in Germany that various universities, schools, and associations asked us to deliver lectures using the panels.

Joerg Fiebelkorn and I were best suited to give the lectures: Joerg as the translator of Michael Good's book and I as one of the 0.5% of Vilna survivors who speak German.

Seven or eight lectures took place between 2006 and 2010 at the following places:

- Ludwig-Georg Gymnasium in Darmstadt, where Plagge studied (an audience of 100 students and teachers);
- A school in Darmstadt whose director is Manfred's wife, Doris Foehr (about 70 students);
- Torgau Castle (two sessions: one for students in the morning and another for adults in the afternoon);
- University of Mainz (30 students, including Jana Müller, director of AJZ (*Alternatives Jugendzentrum*) in Dessau).

With my friend
Joerg Fiebelkorn (right)

I shall never forget the remarkable Jana and her devotion. Not only did she arrange for several conferences in different cities for us, but she also made a film with some survivors. Moreover, she traveled to Eastern Europe to show Nazi extermination camps to young Germans. On one of those trips, to Vilnius, Joerg Fiebelkorn joined a group of young people.

- Prettin in Lichtenburg Castle, a former Nazi prison (a morning session in front of 90 students aged 16-20, followed in the afternoon by a lecture with 30 adults and a few military officers);
- Gedenkstätte Roter Ochse in Halle (60 students and their teachers).

During these lectures, several students asked me if I hated Germans. My answer was: "Why should I hate you for what your grandfather or neighbor did?" Then in turn I asked: "How many Jews do you think were there in Germany before the war?" Answers varied between one and two million. They were surprised when I told them that there had been only 500,000 Jews in Germany,

Left: Lecture in Mainz.

Right: Screening of Jana Müller's film before the lecture. From right to left: Joerg, Jana, and I.

which corresponded to about 0.6% of the population. Furthermore, German Jews were not only perfectly integrated, but there were also many scientists, doctors, writers, and composers among them. The students were astonished to learn this.

Few people know that Jews represent 0.2% of the world population and that their share of Nobel Prizes for contributions to humanity's economic, scientific, and cultural progress is 22%. Many centuries ago, Jews also gave the modern world monotheism.

In 2011, we lost three of our dear friends, who were very active members of our group and whom we miss very much. They were a great help to us and we shall never forget them: Marianne Viefhaus, Joerg Fiebelkorn, and Bill Begell.

Appendix

Karl Plagge's Letter to His Wife, Anke

June 21, 1944

Mein Kosename,[17]

My very pessimistic state of mind is the result of all that has occurred to me here and is possibly related to my health, too. You know, my dear, that I cannot share with you what I see, hear, or experience here. My health is bad as well, but I don't want to talk about that either. There isn't a single man I could speak to among my superiors or my subordinates. I don't share my collaborators' defeatism, nor do I understand my commander's "I don't care" attitude. I'm therefore alone, all by myself, closed within myself. I perform my duty and much more than that with a silent, speechless relentlessness. I know that you, my dear, are much braver, more faithful, and more confident and that you do not understand me. If we could talk, you would maybe be able to judge better how I feel and why I feel this way…. I'm in a different world here. It's the dark and anchorless world of the east. Only a few brief words from me can reach you. The world of my thoughts and judgments is shaped by events, experiences, and the awareness of things that I can neither write, nor want to talk to you about. And yet my entire attitude is determined by them.

Life is heavy, very heavy. Sometimes I think I cannot deal with it but I always struggle through and go on. Reason, feelings,

---

[17] Literally, "pet name."

and physical condition often trip each other up. There is always a strong sense of humanity that arises in me in contrast with the many inhumanities committed around me. This is what is causing the greatest conflict in me. As a National-Socialist, I'm supposed to consent to the massacres and the policy against Poles, a policy according to which they are an inferior category of people and much more.

As a human being, I can clearly see that this is insane and that it will all end up in a heap of rubble because again and again it leads to most violent outbursts. I have been living in the East and working with these people for three years now. Few among them have had as many opportunities to get to know the easterner's psyche. My heart is bleeding: my whole life and energy lies in my work. For it is all my achievement. This life-work rests entirely upon me and it will collapse when I won't be here anymore. It is built upon my sense of humanity, my concern and ideas about what it means to live together. It is part of my nature, of the fulfilment of my existence. No one knows of the difficulty, the struggle, and the conflicts that this organization has brought upon me and continues to cause me every day. The worst conflict is that it all goes against what commanders, or masters, look for and wish for, that is, to erect barriers, use the whip and make its presence felt, place the East under a yoke, and subject us. Such is the policy in the East. That's why they send the scum here: it is just good enough to impress these dirty Polish imps. And yet, I see things completely differently! Do you think I could have made 2000 men work and be indispensable for the Wehrmacht if I believed in those principles? These people work willingly and almost enjoy what they are doing for they know that I'm there to help and protect them. These people were at first wounded, distrustful, dressed in rags, nearly starved to death, and in a state of acute distress from which they still haven't come out. I do what I have to do, I act as my conscience tells me, not because I'm a National Socialist, but despite the fact that I'm a National

Socialist. How painful it is for me to have to tell you all that and how unlikely it is that I find the right words. The Germans' image has suffered so indescribably here due to inapt measures, inept men, contradictory policy, and mismanagement. How humiliating is everything one sees here. All Germans are gritting their teeth.

So many of us are so profoundly ashamed of the stand-off in which we find ourselves. I shall tell you about all this in detail one day, so that you can understand me at least a little. I don't talk or write to anybody about my observations. They weigh on my soul like hidden, heavy stones that no one here even knows exist. They lie heavily on my chest at night and steal my breath and sleep. My dear, I can see you shake your dear head: "Why is he making his life so difficult? Why isn't he different?" Indeed, my dear, why am I that way? Why should things be this way? Why don't I make my life easier, like so many others here? The reason is that, as a senior National Socialist, I feel responsible for what is happening. Because each finger pointed at Germans with disdain also points at me. Because when I find myself among the ruins of a past ideal, those ruins are the debris of my heart. The wound is ever bleeding and painful and it will continue to bleed and hurt as long I live.

...

It is late at night and I'm so tired because a tempest is approaching after a stifling day.

Your Karl

• *Author's Commentary*
Plagge's letter to his wife, Anke, perfectly renders his thoughts and state of mind.

The letter is dated June 21, 1944, that is, only a few days before the HKP camp was evacuated and three weeks before the Red Army's arrival. At the end of June, Plagge gathered everyone in the camp and announced his relocation to the west, saying that he regretted not being able to take us with him. He pointed out that from then on the SS were going to take care of us as they had always done with Jewish forced workers. The signal he gave us was invaluable, telling in a concealed yet clear manner of the camp's imminent liquidation.

Karl Plagge's Letter to the Greisdorf Family

Neunkirchen, February 20, 1948

Qualified Engineer Karl Plagge
Neunkirchen im Odenwald
Via Darmstadt-Land

Dear Herr Greisdorf,

How strange and mysterious are the roads along which life takes us. I constantly think and dream about the people I used to be so close to at that difficult time: where could the people who have grown so dear to my heart be today? Who among my friends has managed to escape from the horror and the hell of this war and has remained alive? Who of them all has escaped the demons of those painful and horrible years that we all had to witness? I was deeply shocked when I read "The Confessions of a Survivor" (*Passover Book 5706* [1946]) by Dr. Mark Dworzecki from Wilno, who survived many concentration camps by miracle. How much courage and how big a heart were necessary not to give up on life and how much I admired you and often almost envied your courage and the reciprocal loyalty you shared.

You, dear Herr Greisdorf, are known to me by name, yet no longer by face. It's a miracle that we are about to meet again and it would be deep and heartfelt joy for me to meet with you once again, that is, if I don't remind you too much of what surely must have been the most terrible part of your life. Frau Dr. Zanker told me, via Frau Eichamüller, that you have been looking for me to thank me for the unfortunately little help I could offer you. Let me tell you then this. What I was able and allowed to do for you and your friends was only what any man should do: help his fellow human beings in distress. But it is also far too little considering the horrible situation in which all found ourselves at the time. No gratitude is required. Yet there is—I am convinced—an inner connection between people who have suffered and whose fates have once crossed. Even if you and yours have suffered a thousand times more than me, I have also suffered during as well as after the war. I believe that only people afflicted by suffering can truly understand each other. In this sense, Herr Greisdorf, our meeting could bring us both great inner joy.

I wrote to Frau Dr. Zanker, who will be so kind to let you know about the possibility of meeting in Stuttgart or Darmstadt. Until then, I remain yours sincerely,

Karl Plagge

Simon Malkes's Speech in Darmstadt, 2005

Very Honored Ladies and Gentlemen,

It is such a joy for a Holocaust survivor to come to Germany and meet people—some for the first time—that I have the feeling are long-time friends. I should therefore add "my dear friends."

Allow me to introduce myself in a few words. My name is Simon Malkes. I live in Paris and am retired. I was born in Wilno in 1927. In 1939, the Russians occupied Eastern Poland and sent my father to prison as a capitalist.

In 1941, the Germans invaded the city, freed my father, and several months later confined us in the ghetto. During the German occupation, my father and I worked as electricians at the HKP 562 workshop for the repairing of military vehicles. From 1943 onward, we lived in the HKP buildings on Subocz Street.

About three to four months before the Red Army's arrival, Karl Plagge took my mother to the city hospital where she had an operation. She remained at the hospital until liberation. This deed made it possible for Yad Vashem to bestow the title Righteous Among the Nations on Plagge in 2005 in Jerusalem.

As soon as we moved to the HKP camp, my father and his friends began building a hideout at night, somewhere we could hide when the time came for the camp to be liquidated. Indeed, we survived thanks to this hideout.

After liberation, we moved to Lodz, Poland, where I took my high-school diploma and studied engineering for two years. In 1949, I transferred to the University of Technology, Munich, where I earned my engineering degree in 1952.

About ten years later, I was working and writing my thesis at the same time. My subject was sampling or ultrafast electronics. I earned my PhD in engineering from the University of Strasbourg. I am married with one daughter and two grandchildren. My parents died sixteen years ago.

There is a saying in all languages, which fits well our event today: better later than never.

Why should it be too late for a group of survivors to remember Karl Plagge's heroism? No, it is never too late to show to the world that in a hateful and violent time, while soldiers' behavior was inhuman, there were some, albeit very few, who had human feelings and could say a kind word, hold out a hand of friendship, and smile.

Yes, Karl Plagge was our hero. In Yiddish, I would have said a *Mentsh*, a man. His subordinates behaved decently as well.

Karl Plagge was an engineer from the TH in Darmstadt. He was also a very cultivated man, as letters sent to HKP survivors after the war demonstrate (his letters to the Greisdorfs and to lawyer Strauss, to give just two examples).

Yad Vashem in Jerusalem was created, among other things, to honor people like him at the time when Jews were condemned to death and their culture and traditions were being erased from the surface of the earth.

The Nazis' mass murder was unprecedented due to its sheer scale. We can infer from it that this, unfortunately, is what human nature is. Historians should ask themselves the following question: what is history's purpose? What does humankind learn from history? Or is history merely the domain of professionals, collecting facts and dates?

Jews have never and nowhere had, throughout their entire history, a peaceful existence as a people, not even today in their own country. Over its 56 years of existence, Israel has suffered five wars and even if Israel has won them all, peace was never really achieved.

It is difficult to protect oneself from kamikazes and snipers, which is why Israel had to build a wall to protect its population. It was not for ideological reasons, but rather to protect lives.

I am not asking for help to protect Israel or help it survive. All I am asking is that Europe ceases criticizing and accusing Israel, whether it be in Brussels, New York, or the UN.

Where do Israeli Jews who have conquered, built, and continue defending this country come from? They are for the most part Holocaust survivors from Europe.

In his letter to Dr Strauss, Karl Plagge refers to Albert Camus's *The Plague*. In this context, I would like to suggest Viviane Forrester's *Western Crime*.

If it were not for the United States, Europeans would have condemned Israel to the UN. To name just a couple of countries: is it possible to compare France and Germany? Two hundred years of history tie France to Arab countries whose citizens have fought for France and until recently were big clients of the arms industry. If this is not the case with Germany, how can one explain the fact that Germany's foreign policy follows in the same line as France's?

We could talk about it for a long time and even ask ourselves the question…if this subject were related to ours. As you know well, when there is a topic that means a lot to you, it is best to give it a voice and the right audience for that is not easy to find.

Thank you for your attention.

Letter from the President of ORT France

My dear Simon,

Marc Timsit gave me your book. I immediately went through it before reading it carefully with great interest and above all an intense emotion.

I can see that you are a miracle man, a child that has escaped from the Nazi horror under absolutely incredible circumstances.

So it was a Wehrmacht officer, who showed humanity and compassion for you and your family. His presence has made it possible for you to talk about the tragedy you were part of.

The uniqueness of your exceptional life deserves to be transmitted to younger generations that have become nowadays increasingly ignorant about our past as Jews.

What it took was meeting a man in uniform, and an enemy at that. But he was above all a good man. You made him a Righteous.

Grace be given to you, my dear Simon.

I would like to express our joy to have you among us and salute you with affectionate friendship,

Lucien Kalfon

Acknowledgements

I would like to express my sincere gratitude to my friend Muriel Chochois, who lives in Lille, France, for her help and precious advice while I was writing this book.

Muriel's great interest in Wilno's rich Jewish culture has taken her on many study trips to that city. Her main focus is the ghetto's medical staff, which looked after the hospital and the orphanage with professionalism and dedication. Muriel devoted herself to studying Dr Schabad-Gawronska's life, studies, and work in particular. Gawronska did not wish to abandon the orphans and accompanied them to Ponary.

My sincere gratitude also goes to my friends and neighbors Jacqueline and Jean Kudela for their help and encouragement to publish this book and thus be able to leave a testimony to future generations.

My warm thanks to my dear friend Dr. Beate Kosmala from Gedenkstätte Deutscher Widerstand (Memorial German Resistance) Berlin for translating my book from French into German, finding an editor and organizing the promotion in Berlin and Darmstadt on June 2014.

Index

Achamer-Pifrader, Humbert 92
Adenauer, Konrad 69
Agynski, Alice 82
Agynski, Marianne — see Funk, Marianne.
Agynski, Paul 67, 68, 69, 71, 73, 80, 82
Alvey, Don 76, 77
American Jewish Joint Distribution Committee 59, 60, 62, 64, 66
Amselem, William 80, 82
Amsterdam 78, 79
Ankstoji Street, Vilnius 27
Arad, Yitzhak 42, 44, 46
Armbruster, prof. 74
Austria 77, 78
Bad Ems, Germany 70
Badasz, Boris 25, 26, 57, 62, 70
Badasz, Fradl 19, 26
Badasz, Grisza 20, 25, 26, 57, 59, 69
Badasz, Kiva 19, 24–26
Badasz, Liza 70
Badasz, Mania — see Wojczyk, Mania.
Badasz, Rasia — see Malkes, Rasia.
Badasz, Riwa 57, 69
Badasz, Senia 57, 58, 70
Badasz, Yuli 25, 26, 57, 70
Begell, Bill 52, 93, 98
Belarus 27, 29–31
Belgium 25, 51, 57, 58, 62, 69
Benz, Peter 93
Berlin 60, 62, 107

Besançon, France 74
Betar Movement, right-wing Zionist organization 21, 80
Billet, Charles 74
Bloch, Jules 80, 82
Brancowskaja, Fania (née Yocheles) 27, 44, 46
Brussels 25, 27, 62, 70, 73, 76, 105
Bulgaria 23
Calvo, Luis 77
Camus, Albert 91, 105
Canada 51, 90
Casip-Cojasor Foundation 66
Champs Elysées, Paris 72
Chochois, Muriel 107
Ciasna Street, Vilnius 19, 27
Côte d'Azur 68
Czechoslovakia 55
Dagin, one of survivors 55
Dagorno, rue, Paris 80
Dantzig 45
Darmstadt 88, 92, 93, 96, 103, 104, 107
Degutis, Darius 95
Delaitre, mr. 68
Deschwanden, Alfons von 93
Deschwanden, Irmgard von 93
Dessau 96
Doyle, Frank 76, 77
Dreyfus, Gilbert 80, 82
Dworzecki, Mark 40, 102
Eichamüller, Frau 90, 102
Endecja, Polish nationalist party (Narodowa Demokracja in Polish, ND) 22

England 23
Esterowicz, Perela 53, 6, 183
Estonia 30, 44
Farber, Rabbi 87
Fiebelkorn, Joerg 88, 89, 94, 96–98
Fis, André 68
Fis, Boris 68
Foehr, Doris 96
Foehr, Manfred 94, 96
Forrester, Viviane 105
FPO (*Fareynikte Partizaner
    Organizatsye*) 42, 44
Fraenkel, Daniel 92
France 23, 27, 28, 58–61, 67, 68, 71,
    74, 77, 105
Funk, Charles 73
Funk, Marianne (née Agynski) 73
Gammer, Wehrmacht soldier 42,
    47, 48, 52
Gdud (then Good), Wowka 61, 83
General Jewish Labor Bund 21
Genichowicz, Assia (née Singer)
    61, 62
Genichowicz, Bomka 61, 62
Gens, Jacob 36, 37, 39, 42, 43
Germany 23, 30, 45, 51, 59–62, 64,
    67, 70, 77, 78, 103, 105
Good, Michael 53, 61, 83, 87, 89,
    92, 96
Goods, family 87
Greisdorf, family 37, 42, 49, 51, 90,
    102, 103, 104
Greisdorf, Lazar 51, 90
Groom, Bob 76
Guernsey 76
Günzburg, Horace de 61
Gutman, Shmuel 53, 55
Hashomer Hatzair, Socialist-
    Zionist organization 21
Haymann, Gérard 72, 73
Hazanovsky, Fruma 45
Herzl, Theodor 21
Hesse, family 89

Hesse, Konrad 89, 90, 92
Hesse, Kurt 89
Heymann, Brigitte (née Weil) 74
Heymann, Gérard 74
Hingst, Hans 36
Hirsch, Maurice de 43
Hitler, Adolf 26, 62, 91, 93
Holszany 14, 15, 18, 19, 23, 25,
    27–29, 31, 45
Hupert, Cesia 65
Hupert, Mark 64, 65
Israel, State of 23, 45, 55, 58, 61, 62,
    69, 70, 73, 77, 80, 87, 93, 95,
    96, 105
Italy 61, 77
Jabotinsky, Ze'ev
Jerusalem 52, 83, 92, 93, 104, 105
Jetter, Christoph 91, 96
Joint Committee—see American
    Jewish Joint Distribution
    Committee.
Kaczerginski, Shmerke 39, 44,
    44n15
Kalfon, Lucien 82, 106
Kaplan, Miron 71
Katyn 32
Kaunas, Lithuania 30
Kerr, Arnold (Kerszkowski
    Arontchik) 63–65
Kerr, Berta 65
Kittel, Bruno 36
KKL (Jewish National Fund) 80
Klaczko, Salomon 88, 89
Kletskin, Boris 21
Klok, Avreml 49
Klok, Rachel 41n13, 42, 49
Kloks, family 37, 42, 49, 51, 52
Kosmala, Beate 107
Koster, Clara 80
Koster, Jean-Michel 80
Koster, Jeremy 80
Koster, Nathalie (née Malkes) 74,
    79, 80

Kowner, Abba 42
Kramer, Harry 72, 73
Kramers, family 73
Kruk, Herman 39
Krupoves, Maria 39n12
Kudela, Jacqueline 107
Kudela, Jean 107
Landis, John 78
Lapidus, Luba (née Malkes) 19, 26, 35
Lapidus, Max 26, 35
Lapidus, Sofia 36
Las Vegas 76
Latvia 30, 43–45, 57, 92
Lazar, Lucien 92
Leopold-Metzger, Jean-Hugues 80
Lerner, Micheline 73
Lerner, Roger 73
Levitan, Yuri 58
Libo 40
Lieberman, Juzek 64
Lille, France 107
Lithuania 58
Lodz, Poland 46, 56, 58–60, 62, 67, 104
London 14, 62, 72, 76
Ludwigsburg, near Stuttgart 90
Lukiszki Square, Vilnius19, 35, 85
Lyon, France 76
Madrid 77
Madsen, Anke 88
Madsen, dr. 91, 92
Mafarette, Francis 71, 72
Magdebourg, Germany 45
Mainke, prof. 63
Malet, Denise (née Milezkowski) 26, 27, 95, 96
Malkes, Abram 14, 26
Malkes, Francine (née Levy) 73, 74, 76, 79
Malkes, Gerszon (Gershon) 19, 26
Malkes, Hinda 26
Malkes, Luba (Lyuba)—see Lapidus, Luba.

Malkes, Nathalie—see Koster, Nathalie.
Malkes, Rasia (née Badasz) 14, 17, 26
Malkes, Simon 26
Margolis, Rachel 39, 42, 46
Max, father's associate 66, 67
Max-Joseph-Platz, Munich 62
Meier, Herbert 51
Meier, Reitz 51
Mexico 57
Mickiewicz Boulevard, Vilnius 17, 19
Mizrachi, religious Zionist organization 21
Möhlstrasse, Munich 62
Montevideo 88
Montrouge, near Paris 69
Moscow 30, 57, 58, 70
Müller, Jana 96–98
Munich 59–64, 68
Napoleon Bonaparte 12, 20
Netherlands 78, 79
New York 40, 64, 71, 105
New York State 87
Nice, France 76
Nissen, Georges 68, 69
NKVD (People's Commissariat for Internal Affairs) 30–32
Novak, Wehrmacht soldier 42, 47
NSDAP (*National Sozialistische Deutsche Arbeiter Partei,* the Nazi Party) 89, 90
Odessa, SU 27
Offenburg, Germany 93
ORT (Association for the Promotion of Skilled Trades) 21, 61, 62, 64, 80, 82, 87
Paldiel, dr. 92
Paleckis, Justas 30
Palestine 21, 23
Paris 14, 27, 45, 62, 64, 66, 67, 72, 73, 76, 78–80, 92, 103

Parisier, Maurice 71, 72, 74
Pilsudski, Joseph 22
Plagge, Anke 91, 99, 101
Plagge, Karl 12, 42, 43, 51, 52, 83,
      85–92, 94, 96, 99, 101–105
Poland 24, 29, 35, 59, 60, 63, 64
Ponary 35, 37, 43, 44, 52, 54, 83, 85,
      94–96, 107
Portland, Oregon 64, 71, 76, 79
Puteaux, France 69
Ranelagh, rue du, Paris 74
Rebibo, Jacqueline 92
Richter, SS officer 45, 49
Riga 43, 57, 92
Riwkes, family 23, 31–33, 57, 58,
      62, 69
Rome 61
Romm, family 21
Rothschilds 66n16
Roubach, Eliane 80, 82
Rovno 26, 29, 34, 70
Rudnicka Street, Vilnius 32, 36
Russia 34, 62
Saint Petersburg 61, 62
Saint-Germain-des-Pres, Paris 72
Sakins, survivors family 58
Sceaux, near Paris 73
Schabad-Gawronska, dr. 40, 107
Schemiavitz, Michael 93
Schleiden, Germany 91
Schneerson, Boris 80, 82
Schulman, Charles 72
Sedlis 40
Shalev, Avner 92, 93
Shapiro, family 27, 28
Shapiro, Meier 45, 59
Shevelovitch-Katz, mrs. 16
Siberia 23, 31, 32, 33, 57, 58
Simaite, Anna 39
Singer, Ida 61
Singers, family 61
Skroblies, Hanni (Hannelore) 90,
      91, 96

Slowacki Street, Vilnius 19, 27
Solzhenitsyn, Aleksandr 57
Soviet Union 23, 62, 70
Spain 73, 77, 78
Stalin, I, V. 26, 31, 32, 58, 70
Stern, Jacob (Kuba) 64
Strasbourg 80, 93
Strauss, a lawyer 91, 104, 105
Stuttgart 103
Subocz Street, Vilnius 43, 47, 48,
      49, 56, 83, 85, 95, 103
Sutzkewer, Avrom 39, 44, 44n15
Swirsky, David 87
Swirsky, Marek 87
Switzerland 57
Taboryski, Samuel 93
Tarrel, mr. 68
Tatarska Street, Vilnius 56
Tel Aviv 62, 55, 95
Timsit, Marc 82, 106
Toulouse, France 76
Treche, general 94
Trocka Street, Vilnius 16
Trocki, Saul 35
Turgel, Asia 45
Ukraine 29, 30
Ulis, near Paris 75
United Kingdom 60
United States 23, 43, 45, 52, 59–62,
      64, 76, 83, 93, 105
United Nations (UN) 105
Viefhaus, Marianne 88–90, 98
Vienna 70, 78
Vignes, rue des, Paris 74
Vilnius (Wilno, Vilna) 12, 14, 15,
      18, 20– 27, 29–32, 34, 35,
      42, 44–46, 49, 55–59, 61, 66,
      67, 79, 83, 85, 87, 88, 91, 93,
      95–97, 102, 103, 107
Volum, Howard 71
Warsaw 23
Washington DC 64
Weis, Derek 77

Weis, Maria-Grazia 78
Weiss, Martin 36
Wette, Wolfram 93
Wittenberg, Yitzhak 42
Woerner, Johann-Dietrich 93
Wojczyk (Woitchik) Maurice 26, 57, 58, 62, 70, 73
Wojczyk, Boris 69
Wojczyk, family 34, 57, 58, 62, 70
Wojczyk, Mania (née Badasz) 25, 26, 58, 69, 70
Wojczyk, Samuel 26, 58
Wrobel, Marianne 94–96

Yad Vashem 42, 83, 92, 93, 95, 104, 105
Yagmin 15, 16, 28, 31
YIVO (Yiddish Scientific Institute; YIVO Institute for Jewish Research, New York) 22, 39, 40
Zaidel, one of survivors 55
Zalkind, family
Zanker, dr. 102, 103
Zawalna Street, Vilnius 14

Lightning Source UK Ltd.
Milton Keynes UK
UKOW06f1428150115

244543UK00003B/22/P